2000

100 WORKS BY MODERN MASTERS FROM THE GUGGENHEIM MUSEUM

W9-BWL-301

University of St. Francis Library

3 0301 00208173 1

100 WORKS BY MODERN MASTERS FROM THE GUGGENHEIM MUSEUM

100 WORKS BY MODERN MASTERS

FROM THE GUGGENHEIM MUSEUM

Text by VIVIAN ENDICOTT BARNETT

Curator, The Solomon R. Guggenheim Museum

Introduction and Selection by THOMAS M. MESSER

Director, The Solomon R. Guggenheim Foundation

LIBRARY
UNIVERSITY OF ST. FRANCIS
JOLIET, ILLINOIS

Harry N. Abrams, Inc., Publishers, New York

Project Director: Margaret L. Kaplan
Editors: Carol Fuerstein, The Solomon R. Guggenheim Museum
        Sheila Franklin, Harry N. Abrams, Inc.
Designer: Bob McKee

Library of Congress Cataloging in Publication Data
Main entry under title:

100 works by modern masters from the Guggenheim Museum.

Includes index.
1. Art, Modern—20th century.   2. Art—New York
(N.Y.) 3. Solomon R. Guggenheim Museum.   4. Solomon R.
Guggenheim Foundation.   I. Barnett, Vivian Endicott.
II. Messer, Thomas M.   III. Solomon R. Guggenheim
Museum.   IV. Title: One hundred works by modern masters
from the Guggenheim Museum.
N6487.N4S6383 1984   709'.04'00740471   83-15512
ISBN 0-8109-0370-9
ISBN 0-8109-2281-9 (pbk.)

Illustrations © 1984 The Solomon R. Guggenheim Foundation, New York
Published in 1984 by Harry N. Abrams, Incorporated, New York
All rights reserved. No part of the contents of this book
may be reproduced without the written permission of the publishers

Picture reproduction rights reserved by S. P. A. D. E. M.
and A. D. A. G. P., Paris, where relevant

Printed and bound in Italy by Amilcare Pizzi S.p.A., Milan

Note to the reader: This book has been organized according to
essentially stylistic, art-historical designations. The arrangements
are not strictly chronological, since all works by one artist have
been kept together. Artists of the same generation and sometimes of
the same nationality have been grouped together. A maximum of
three works by a single artist has been included. Any selection of
masterpieces from a museum's permanent collection is
interpretative and can only suggest the depth and richness of the
institution's holdings.

769.04
B259

CONTENTS

1861 Birth of Solomon R. Guggenheim.

1893 Birth of Harry F. Guggenheim (Solomon's nephew).

1895 Marriage of Solomon R. Guggenheim to Irene Rothschild.

1898 Birth of Peggy Guggenheim (Solomon's niece).

1912 Benjamin Guggenheim (Peggy's father) goes down with the *Titanic*.

1920 Eleanor Guggenheim (Solomon's daughter) marries Lord Castle-Stewart.

1921 Peggy Guggenheim leaves the United States for Europe.

1925 Barbara Guggenheim (Solomon's daughter) marries John Robert Lawson-Johnston.

1927 Birth of Peter O. Lawson-Johnston (Solomon's grandson).

Hilla Rebay von Ehrenwiesen arrives in the United States from Germany; meets Solomon R. Guggenheim; begins to acquire modern paintings for his private collection.

1937 The Solomon R. Guggenheim Foundation is incorporated in the State of New York and endowed to operate the Museum of Non-Objective Painting.

Solomon R. Guggenheim is elected first President of the Foundation; Hilla Rebay is elected Trustee of the Foundation and appointed Curator.

1938 Peggy Guggenheim opens commercial art gallery, Guggenheim Jeune, in London; begins to collect modern art in Paris.

1939 Museum of Non-Objective Painting opens at 24 East 54th Street.

Hilla Rebay is appointed first Director of the Museum.

1941 Peggy Guggenheim returns to the United States.

1942 Peggy Guggenheim marries Max Ernst; opens commercial art gallery, Art of This Century, in New York.

1943 Solomon R. Guggenheim commissions Frank Lloyd Wright to design museum.

Peggy Guggenheim and Max Ernst divorce.

1946 Peggy Guggenheim closes Art of This Century and returns to Europe for good.

1947 Museum of Non-Objective Painting moves to 1071 Fifth Avenue.

1949 Peggy Guggenheim buys the Palazzo Venier dei Leoni in Venice; opens her collection to the public; establishes The Peggy Guggenheim Foundation.

Solomon R. Guggenheim dies.

1950 Lord Castle-Stewart is elected second President of the Foundation.

1951 Lord Castle-Stewart resigns; Harry F. Guggenheim is elected third President of the Foundation.

1952 Hilla Rebay resigns as Director of the Museum and is named Director Emeritus; James Johnson Sweeney is appointed second Director of the Museum.

Name "Museum of Non-Objective Painting" is changed to "The Solomon R. Guggenheim Museum."

Carl Zigrosser is elected Trustee of the Foundation, thus becoming first Museum professional on the Foundation Board.

Lord Castle-Stewart dies.

1956 Construction of the Wright building begins at 1071 Fifth Avenue; Museum moves temporarily to 7 East 72nd Street.

1959 Frank Lloyd Wright dies.

The Solomon R. Guggenheim Museum opens in Wright building on Fifth Avenue.

1960 James Johnson Sweeney resigns as Director of the Museum.

Daniel Catton Rich is elected Trustee of the Foundation.

H. Harvard Arnason is elected Trustee of the Foundation and the Foundation's Vice-President for Art Administration.

1961 Thomas M. Messer is appointed third Director of the Museum.

1963 Justin K. Thannhauser makes permanent loan to the Foundation of part of his collection.

1964 Peter O. Lawson-Johnston is elected Trustee of the Foundation.

1965 Justin K. Thannhauser Wing opens at The Solomon R. Guggenheim Museum.

1966 Peter O. Lawson-Johnston is elected the Foundation's Vice-President for Business Administration.

1967 Hilla Rebay dies.

1968 Completion of annex to the main building of the Museum by the Frank Lloyd Wright Foundation.

1969 Carl Zigrosser dies.

H. Harvard Arnason retires as the Foundation's Vice-President for Art Administration.

Harry F. Guggenheim retires as President of the Foundation to become Chairman of the Board; Peter O. Lawson-Johnston is elected fourth President of the Foundation.

The Peggy Guggenheim Collection is shown at The Solomon R. Guggenheim Museum.

1970 Peggy Guggenheim deeds her collection to the custody of The Solomon R. Guggenheim Foundation.

1971 The Hilla von Rebay Foundation and The Solomon R. Guggenheim Foundation divide works of art left in the Estate of Hilla Rebay.

Harry F. Guggenheim dies.

1972 Reinstallation of the Justin K. Thannhauser Wing on occasion of donor's eightieth birthday.

1976 Justin K. Thannhauser dies.

The Peggy Guggenheim Collection becomes Italian National Monument; Peggy Guggenheim Foundation is dissolved; legal transfer of The Peggy Guggenheim Collection and the Palazzo Venier dei Leoni to The Solomon R. Guggenheim Foundation.

1977 The Solomon R. Guggenheim Foundation celebrates fortieth anniversary; Nina Kandinsky is guest of honor.

First publication of Annual Report.

Inauguration of Half-Century Fund Drive.

Daniel Catton Rich dies.

1978 Seymour Slive is elected Trustee of the Foundation.

1979 Peggy Guggenheim dies.

Palazzo Venier dei Leoni and The Peggy Guggenheim Collection are taken into Foundation custody.

Thomas M. Messer is charged with directorship of The Peggy Guggenheim Collection.

1980 Reinstalled Peggy Guggenheim Collection opens in Venice.

Opening of permanent collection gallery Pioneers of Twentieth-Century Art at The Solomon R. Guggenheim Museum.

Thomas M. Messer is appointed first Director of The Solomon R. Guggenheim Foundation in recognition of his double directorship of The Solomon R. Guggenheim Museum and The Peggy Guggenheim Collection; also elected Trustee of the Foundation.

HISTORY OF THE COLLECTION

The Guggenheims who shaped this Foundation and its two museums in New York and in Venice were born within little more than half a century. They span three generations, from Solomon R. Guggenheim, the founding benefactor, to Peter O. Lawson-Johnston, his grandson, the Foundation's current President. Between the two extremes lie the birthdays of the late Harry F. Guggenheim, the founder's nephew, and Peggy Guggenheim, whose own Foundation has recently been absorbed by her uncle's.

The period between the birth of the older Guggenheims in the late nineteenth century and that of the current generation encompasses one of the grand epics of modern capitalism, which is described in all its fascinating detail in a number of recent books on the subject. The common theme of these stories is the amassing of great family wealth leading, in due course, to organized philanthropy and the creation of tax-exempt, nonprofit institutions with a diversity of purposes. The Guggenheim brothers, each in his own manner, exemplified this socioeconomic pattern, and one of them, Solomon, placed his Foundation's wealth at the service of a museum dedicated to modern art.

*　　*　　*

The decisive years that led to the creation of the Guggenheim museums as we know them are roughly 1927 to 1949—a period that happens to begin with the birth of the Foundation's current President and end with the death of its founder—for it is within these years that the passionate collecting of two great ladies launched two modern museums on separate, but equally influential, paths. First on the scene was Hilla Rebay, a

Solomon R. Guggenheim

Left to right: Irene Guggenheim, Vasily Kandinsky,
Hilla Rebay, Solomon R. Guggenheim,
at the Bauhaus, Dessau, 1930

Harry F. Guggenheim

Hilla Rebay

German baroness and gifted painter, who, upon her arrival in the United States in 1927, became Solomon R. Guggenheim's muse as well as the stormy petrel of nonobjective painting. A decade later Peggy Guggenheim, Solomon's "poor" self-exiled niece, aided by sophisticated members of the art world in Europe and America, embarked on her own tastemaking, first in London and Paris and then, during the war years, via her gallery in New York. The tangible result of Hilla Rebay's striving was the Museum of Non-Objective Painting, which, under her directorship, eventually became the operative arm of The Solomon R. Guggenheim Foundation. The Museum's original holdings consisted of Solomon's paintings, acquired earlier with Miss Rebay's help and now donated to the newly formed institution, which, for the time being, was lodged in modest quarters refurbished for the purpose. The grand spiral monument that today houses a much enlarged collection was then only an embryonic idea in the mind of architect Frank Lloyd Wright, whom Solomon commissioned, upon Rebay's advice, to design the present building. Peggy Guggenheim's collection, initially comprising European art but significantly enriched by American works acquired during her New York gallery days, was installed in a handsome eighteenth-century palazzo on the Grand Canal in Venice. With the death of Solomon R. Guggenheim in 1949, therefore, the elements of the present foundation complex were already in existence, though only partially realized.

Museum of Non-Objective Painting,
24 East 54th Street

Art of This Century gallery, New York, c. 1942

Left to right: Hilla Rebay, Solomon R. Guggenheim,
Frank Lloyd Wright, at luncheon celebrating
plans to build museum, 1943

Installation view, "In Memory of Wassily Kandinsky"
exhibition, Museum of Non-Objective Painting,
24 East 54th Street, 1945

During the 1950s, the Foundation's policies underwent modifications that had far-reaching implications. Hilla Rebay's missionary dogmaticism with respect to nonobjective painting was not shared by the succeeding policy-makers; it was therefore abandoned, partly in favor of a commitment to art education, but also for a broader aesthetic that encompassed both twentieth-century painting and sculpture, and in which quality, irrespective of artistic idiom, became the exclusive criterion. The new course was signaled by the changing of the institution's name from the programmatic "Museum of Non-Objective Painting" to the stylistically neutral "The Solomon R. Guggenheim Museum." The newly baptized museum continued to be operated by the Foundation, thus ensuring administrative continuity despite personnel and policy changes. Under second Director James Johnson Sweeney's professional leadership, an important exhibition program began to attract a small but informed public; in addition, as institutional holdings were enriched by the first donations from outside sources and by important purchases, the scope of Solomon R. Guggenheim's original collection was dramatically extended.

In other respects as well, the decade of the 1950s was a transitional one. While the small museum functioned in temporary quarters, the aged but spirited Frank Lloyd Wright, overcoming difficulties of every kind, pursued his last great project to a triumphant conclusion. After this remarkable tour de force the

Museum of Non-Objective Painting,
1071 Fifth Avenue, c. 1948

Installation view, "Tenth Anniversary Exhibition,"
Museum of Non-Objective Painting,
1071 Fifth Avenue, 1949

Palazzo Venier dei Leoni, Venice

second phase of the Foundation's history came to a close with the decade itself, for in 1959, a few months after Frank Lloyd Wright's death, his extraordinary and controversial architectural milestone opened on Fifth Avenue. James Johnson Sweeney's resignation in 1960 marked the end of an era.

Throughout the 1960s, socioeconomic, organizational, and aesthetic transformations wrought fundamental changes in the Foundation's institutional character. Economic developments that necessitated dependence on outside support and earned income radically decreased the Museum's purchasing power, thereby slowing the collecting process that, from the institution's beginnings, has been its top priority. The newly inaugurated Frank Lloyd Wright building, by virtue of its size and the fascination it held for a large public, provided the stage for spectacular exhibitions. Thomas M. Messer, the Museum's third Director, found ample opportunities to familiarize himself, and a now sizable curatorial and technical staff, with the new and largely untried spaces of the building. Through the staging of major shows that constituted the Museum program of the sixties, the Guggenheim gained an international reputation as a leading exhibition center.

A new order was established toward the end of the decade when the presidency of the Foundation passed from Harry F. Guggenheim to Peter O. Lawson-Johnston, who quickly instituted effective administrative procedures that greatly strengthened the Museum's structure. But while collecting through purchase remained marginal, the collection continued to grow through other means. A series of major gifts and their placement on public view provided the needed momentum. The first of these gifts occurred when the late Justin K. Thannhauser, a leading dealer of Impressionist and modern French painting, agreed to bequeath to the Foundation a generous portion of his private collection of modern masters. More or less contempo-

Frank Lloyd Wright, on the ramp of
unfinished museum building, c. 1958

The Solomon R. Guggenheim Museum,
1071 Fifth Avenue, c. 1959

James Johnson Sweeney, c. 1956

Thomas M. Messer, c. 1962

Installation view, "Vasily Kandinsky 1866–1944: A Retrospective Exhibition,"
The Solomon R. Guggenheim Museum, 1963

Installation view, "Alexander Calder:
A Retrospective Exhibition,"
The Solomon R. Guggenheim Museum, 1964

Peter O. Lawson-Johnston, 1969

raneous with the Thannhauser bequest and its installation in a newly designated wing of the building was the reintegration with the Museum's permanent holdings of one half of the art collection that was left in Hilla Rebay's Estate at the time of her death. Finally, toward the end of the 1970s, the placement into the Foundation's permanent custody of Peggy Guggenheim's Venetian palazzo—containing her entire collection of Cubist, Surrealist, and postwar painting and sculpture—completed the sequence of extraordinary enrichments that occurred during the last two decades.

Three months after Peggy Guggenheim's death in 1979, the Palazzo Venier dei Leoni was reopened in her name. The occasion heralded subsequent presentations designed to highlight her accomplishment as a collector and at the same time to define the relationship of her great gift to the Foundation's collection as a whole. For example, a major show at the Campidoglio in Rome in 1982 brought together for the first time her modern treasures and the New York Museum's finest purchases and gifts.

The absorption of Peggy Guggenheim's collection by The Solomon R. Guggenheim Foundation had additional far-reaching consequences, for the Foundation was now called upon to guide, administer, and finance two related but separate institutions—The Solomon R. Guggenheim Museum in New York, with its roots in the Museum of Non-Objective Painting, and The Peggy Guggenheim Collection in Venice, formed by a Guggenheim whose erstwhile opposition to the family was suspended by the unfathomable progression of events. The result of these developments is a unique phenomenon in the museum world: the parallel functioning of two related institutional organisms on two continents. The collections in both may be enjoyed for their own sakes; but it is their complementary potential, realized at times through exchanges and combined showings, that bestows upon the Guggenheim Foundation collection its fullest significance.

Left to right: Justin K. Thannhauser, Hilde Thannhauser, Harry F. Guggenheim, with model of Justin K. Thannhauser Wing, c. 1963

Justin K. Thannhauser at opening of reinstalled Thannhauser Wing, 1972

Installation view, Justin K. Thannhauser Wing, 1982

Nina Kandinsky and Thomas M. Messer at Museum's fortieth anniversary festivities, 1977

Installation view, Pioneers of Twentieth-Century Art gallery, The Solomon R. Guggenheim Museum, 1980

Peggy Guggenheim, 1970s

Interior, Palazzo Venier dei Leoni, 1982

INTRODUCTION

The collection of The Solomon R. Guggenheim Foundation has been formed over a period of about fifty years by a small number of individuals. Some of these worked in close cooperation with one another, such as Solomon R. Guggenheim, the institution's founder, and Baroness Hilla Rebay, the Museum's first Director; others worked in succession, such as the three Directors who, since the Foundation's creation, determined the collection's main outline; and still others, namely Justin K. Thannhauser and Peggy Guggenheim, formed private collections of their own that they eventually turned over to the Foundation, thereby giving it new dimensions not originally envisaged. Since each of these private and institutional collectors acted according to some concept and since their concepts of collecting, though partially overlapping, were by no means identical or even necessarily compatible, the Foundation's collection as it now appears must be seen as a kind of anthology in which the overall form is derived from the sum of its successive parts. The following pages will attempt to characterize the underlying rationale of each one of these concepts and to provide some information about the conditions that helped or hindered the translation of theoretical notions into recognizable patterns of collecting.

When The Solomon R. Guggenheim Foundation came into existence it assumed control of a privately assembled collection with a distinct stylistic identity. The clearly restrictive notions that guided the formation of the collection were predicated upon an almost mystical belief in the preeminence of "nonobjective painting." The collection so conceived was to consist of works that were self-contained in their formal perfection and therefore not dependent upon recognizable images or traditional subject matter for their meaning. A fine distinction was made between "nonobjective" (a rather inadequate translation of the German *gegenstandslos*—devoid of object) and "abstract." While the latter presumably drew its imagery from an observable reality, as was the case in Cubism, the former avoided even vestigial references to such presumed points of departure. Vasily Kandinsky as of the second decade of our century, Rudolf Bauer, and Hilla Rebay herself were, according to this dogma, the purest spirits of nonobjectivity. But even Cubists such as Picasso, Léger, Gleizes, and Gris, the Orphic Cubist Delaunay, the Futurist Severini, the fantasists Chagall, Klee, and Marc as well as the geometric painters of the Dutch De Stijl and the German Bauhaus found acceptance within the nonobjective pantheon that dominated collection thinking at the Museum in the 1930s and 1940s. Apart from such exceptions as Seurat, Rousseau, and Vuillard, whose work stemmed from an earlier historical period, the chronological span of the Foundation's first phase of collecting encompassed the four decades from 1910 to 1950. The feeling of the Museum of Non-Objective Painting was thus distinctly avant-garde, even though its identification as such was only partially accurate since many of the finest works to enter the Museum in those days were bought with the benefit of one or more decades of hindsight. The results, in any event, were stupendous and remain to this day the basis of the Foundation's collection.

If the first two decades of the Museum's history favored nonobjective painting, the 1950s, under James Johnson Sweeney's artistic leadership, moved the still young and pliable institution in different directions. With the consent of the Trustees, the Museum's name was changed from its original designation to one without stylistic connotation—a clear indication that the dogma of nonobjectivity was giving way to a broader definition of modernism. The new Solomon R. Guggenheim Museum simply sought to acquire modern paintings and sculptures of particular distinction. The purchase of Cézanne's *Man with Crossed Arms* (c. 1899) not only extended the previous chronological expanse back into history by a good decade, but by its conspicuously explicit subject matter it heralded a departure from former stylistic requirements. Similarly, the programmatic acquisition of sculptures by Brancusi, Giacometti, Duchamp-Villon, Moore, and many others asserted the validity of a medium that, because of its corporeality, had previously remained outside of the Museum's collecting scope. What was carried over from the first to this second phase was a commitment to the avant-garde, which, through the passage of time, now came to include works of the 1950s created in America and in Europe. Equally important was the inclusion of key works—previously excluded or overlooked—that had now come to be perceived within a historical framework: examples by Braque,

Picabia, Malevich, and Van Doesburg would be the most prominent among these. In all such instances the collecting goal was excellence of the individual item—quality, in other words, that stood relatively unencumbered by stylistic considerations. The general orientation, however, remained strongly within the reigning abstract mode of the times, one that obviously owed a debt to the pioneer examples of abstract art that had been the Museum's birthright a generation earlier.

The three-pronged goal that came to characterize collecting in the 1950s—deepening of the historical dimension through further extensions into the past, strengthening of contemporary representation through the addition of works by artists not previously included in already established areas, and the attempt to keep up with current and typically younger production—also guided the new administration that took charge under my directorship in the early 1960s and that continues to the present. Thus, Kupka for the first time joined Delaunay in the realm of Orphism, while a painting by Duchamp was ranged next to previously purchased Futurist and Cubist works by Severini and Feininger. A major Jawlensky was added to the collection to balance a preponderance of works by his fellow Russian Kandinsky, and Kirchner, Nolde, Beckmann, as well as Schiele, bolstered a German and Austrian Expressionist presence previously insufficiently indicated by a single, though major, work of Kokoschka. Postwar painting and sculpture from both hemispheres joined earlier comparable acquisitions of the 1950s, thereby creating within the collection a tighter and somewhat more coherent texture. But the single most conspicuous void that had defied all previous corrective efforts would not be filled until two decades later, when the Museum acquired, by exchange with New York's Museum of Modern Art, Matisse's *The Italian Woman* (1916).

For various reasons, collecting from the 1960s onward ceased to revolve around purchasing and relied increasingly on the participatory role of donors/collectors instead. But before describing the part played by donors to the collection, a word about changing conditions underlying collecting itself would seem to be in order.

As has been stated already, the Museum of Non-Objective Painting grew out of a private collection that had been formed during the better part of a decade. Once under public management, the former exclusive concentration upon purchasing inevitably gave way to a degree of institutionalization, but collecting still remained the primary concern of the founding generation. Such activity was financed with yields from the Foundation's capital, which at the time had few other commitments, and therefore remained essentially intact until the costs incurred by the construction of the Frank Lloyd Wright building began to invade and decrease it. The very personal relationships that gave the original collection its coloring and continued when it became a public trust began to give way in the 1950s to an embryonic museum situation, one that by the 1960s had matured into a full-fledged museum organization with an active exhibiting and publishing program. The once preeminent goal of collecting thus had to take its place as one among many of the Museum's activities. The notable surpluses that had formerly been available, even after the modest operating needs were covered, diminished markedly in the 1960s and eventually disappeared entirely, as the Guggenheim, like many other museums, began to show controlled but recurrent annual operating deficits. It is therefore something of a miracle that these unfavorable economic conditions did not eliminate the Guggenheim's traditional collecting aspirations, but that a new mode of collecting came into being in which reliance upon gifts and exchanges gradually superseded the previous method of self-reliant acquisition.

While gifts to the Foundation in some important instances reflected the collecting personality of the donor, they were also not infrequently the result of choices that originated within the Museum—choices that would then be purchased with funds contributed by the Guggenheim's friends, who were growing in number. The collecting process was thus complicated but by no means relegated to outside initiatives. There was still some vestigial buying, and the Museum, its Director, and his curatorial staff also retained a certain degree of latitude through the repeated use of sometimes not insignificant funds generated by the sale of works from the collection. In addition, by reducing what had formerly been super concentrations (the works of Kandinsky, Klee, and Bauer among others) in favor of broader coverage, and by instituting the practice of exchanging lesser works for single masterpieces, the collection continued to diversify and expand.

But to return to the metamorphosis of The Solomon R. Guggenheim Foundation collection and to the crucial part played by collectors, it is appropriate now to introduce the names of Justin K. Thannhauser and Peggy Guggenheim, who together with Solomon R. Guggenheim constituted the donor triad that balanced and complemented the professional tasks of three museum administrations. Both the Thannhauser and the Peggy Guggenheim collections were legally transferred to the Foundation in the 1970s after years of preliminary negotiations and temporary arrangements.

Justin K. Thannhauser's primary attachment was to French painting of the late nineteenth century and to the figurative contingent within the School of Paris that followed. His gift, therefore, contained much that had been lacking among Foundation holdings. Through his donation, works by Picasso and Braque in particular were extended beyond the already well-represented Cubist phase to include earlier and later idioms that clearly stood outside the scope of the founding dogma. Even more important in terms of the Museum's diversification was a gift of Impressionist and Post-Impressionist art that, for the second time now, enlarged the range of the Guggenheim collection while significantly complementing heretofore weak areas. In this instance, the chronology was extended by another twenty years, thus aligning paintings by Cézanne, Van Gogh, Gauguin, Toulouse-Lautrec, and Vuillard with the negligibly small number of Post-Impressionist examples that had previously been acquired. As for the still earlier examples by Pissarro, Manet, Renoir, and Degas, these obviously represented a separate category but at the same time constituted a logical and enjoyable point of departure for the collection as a whole. Indeed, as a result of the Thannhauser gift the Museum could, for the first time in its history, claim to be a treasure house of modern art in the fullest sense—an ambition that was never entertained by the original Museum of Non-Objective Painting, nor even realistically imagined during the immediately succeeding years.

The comprehensiveness of the collection was further enhanced by the absorption of Peggy Guggenheim's Venetian holdings, which were turned over to the custody of The Solomon R. Guggenheim Foundation after a series of legal steps were completed in 1976, three years before the donor's death. It is understood that Peggy Guggenheim's legacy will retain as its legal residence her former palazzo on the Grand Canal, which has also become the Foundation's property; yet the existing and already demonstrated opportunities for mutual exchanges of collections as well as for combined presentations allow us to view the Guggenheim collection in Venice not only as a legacy that bears testimony to the sagacity of an exceptional collector, but also as a new dimension of an enlarged concept for the Guggenheim Foundation collection as a whole. For, in addition to giving the representations of Picasso, Braque, Léger, Mondrian, Malevich, Brancusi, Arp, Giacometti, and Moore, among others, a depth that was undreamed of even a few years ago, Peggy Guggenheim's collection has added decisive examples of Dada and Surrealism from De Chirico and Ernst to Masson and Matta to include virtually all of the great names who, in the twenties, the thirties, and thereafter, provided a vital alternative to Neo-Plastic idealization. If to these one adds the few but telling examples that she originally acquired from artists during the period of her gallery activity in New York, the transfer of her collection to the Guggenheim Foundation emerges before us in its full scope and significance. In its complementary relationship to The Solomon R. Guggenheim Museum, Peggy Guggenheim's achievement as collector comes close to completing an evolution that began by seeing nonobjective painting as the ultimate pictorial expression, only to abandon such faith in favor of a more modest search for qualitative excellence and eventually reach out for a broader definition of modernism that would insist on a measure of art-historical continuity.

At its half-century mark, The Solomon R. Guggenheim Foundation can rejoice at the sight of the acquisitions made by its founding generations; take pride in the process whereby, with the help of hindsight, some of its persisting inadequacies have been corrected; regard with attentive and active interest the gradual jelling of postwar patterns; and leave as free a rein as possible to the intuitions of those now attempting to sort out the kaleidoscopic variety of current production.

Thomas M. Messer, *Director*
The Solomon R. Guggenheim Foundation

COMMENTARIES

Pissarro • Manet • Degas • Renoir • Seurat • Cézanne • Van Gogh • Gauguin • Toulouse-Lautrec • Rousseau •
Vuillard • Bonnard • Maillol • Munch • Matisse • Braque • Picasso • Léger

CAMILLE PISSARRO 1830–1903. Jacob Camille Pissarro was born on July 10, 1830, in Saint Thomas, the Danish West Indies. In Paris in 1855, he briefly attended the Ecole des Beaux-Arts, but preferred the Académie Suisse, where he later met Claude Monet, Paul Cézanne, and Armand Guillaumin. While at the Ecole he met Camille-Jean-Baptiste Corot, whose work impressed him deeply. The Salon in Paris showed his paintings for the first time in 1859. In 1863 Pissarro participated in the Salon des Refusés, which displayed works not accepted by the jury of the official Paris Salon. He moved to Pontoise three years later, when his work again appeared at the Salon and was admired by Emile Zola. Pissarro settled in Louveciennes in 1869 but fled to Brittany and then to England when the Franco-Prussian War broke out the following year. In London he associated with Monet and sold works to the art dealer Paul Durand-Ruel. Pissarro returned to France in 1871, resettling the next year in Pontoise, where he was joined by Cézanne and Guillaumin. He participated in all eight Impressionist exhibitions, from 1874 to 1886. In Pontoise he frequently painted in the company of Cézanne or Paul Gauguin.

Pissarro's first one-man show took place in Paris in 1883 at Durand-Ruel's gallery. He moved in 1884 to Eragny. During the mid-1880s he formed friendships with Vincent and Theo van Gogh, Paul Signac, and Georges Seurat. In 1887 he showed with the progressive group Les XX (Les Vingt) in Brussels and in Georges Petit's Exposition Internationale in Paris. The following year he exhibited at Durand-Ruel's. Durand-Ruel made sizable purchases of his work in 1889, when the artist's eye trouble became severe. In 1890 he again exhibited with Les XX and he visited his son Lucien, also an artist, in London. In 1897 he traveled again to England and took part in the Carnegie International in Pittsburgh, in which he participated annually until 1901. During the last years of his life Pissarro lived primarily in Eragny and Paris, where he died on November 13, 1903.

1. THE HERMITAGE AT PONTOISE. c. 1867
(Les Côteaux de l'Hermitage, Pontoise)
Oil on canvas, 59⅝ × 79 in. (151.4 × 200.6 cm.)
Gift, Justin K. Thannhauser, 1978

Pissarro's large-scale canvas *The Hermitage at Pontoise* dates from about 1867 and thus precedes his Impressionist paintings. He has structured the composition in a traditional manner: an open foreground space functions as a *repoussoir* element, a winding road leads back to the houses in the middle distance, and, finally, a hillside demarcates the background. The artist has positioned nine figures within the landscape to further define an orderly recession into the distance. Not only the conventional device of a road and the utilization of genre figures but, above all, the considerable dimensions—approximately five by six and a half feet—of this picture place it within the tradition of Salon painting. Although it is not possible to determine that *The Hermitage at Pontoise* was exhibited at the Salon of 1868, it certainly looks as if it were painted with that intention. Pissarro maintains clear distinctions between foreground and background, architectural and landscape elements, areas of light and shadow. He achieves a consistent pictorial space: clarity and solidity pervade his landscape.

EDOUARD MANET

1832–1883. Edouard Manet was born on January 23, 1832, in Paris. While studying with Thomas Couture from 1850 to 1856, he drew at the Académie Suisse and copied the old masters at the Louvre. After he left Couture's studio, Manet traveled extensively in Europe, visiting Belgium, the Netherlands, Germany, Austria, and Italy. In 1859 he was rejected by the official Paris Salon, although Eugène Delacroix intervened on his behalf. In 1861 Manet's paintings were accepted by the Salon and received favorable comments in the press, and he began exhibiting at the Galerie Martinet in Paris. During the early 1860s his friendships with Charles Baudelaire and Edgar Degas began. The three paintings Manet sent to the Salon of 1863, including *Le Déjeuner sur l'herbe*, were relegated to the Salon des Refusés, where they attracted the attention of the critic Théophile Thoré.

In 1865 Manet's *Olympia* and *Christ Mocked* were greeted with great hostility when shown at the Salon. That year the painter traveled to Spain, where he met Théodore Duret. He became a friend of Zola in 1866, when the writer defended him in a controversial article for the periodical *L'Evénement*. In 1867 Zola published a longer article on Manet, who that year exhibited his work in an independent pavilion at the Paris World's Fair. The artist spent the first of several summers at Boulogne at this time. In 1868 two of his works were accepted by the Salon but were not shown to advantage.

The dealer Durand-Ruel began buying his work in 1872. That same year *The Battle of the Kearsarge and the Alabama* was shown at the Salon, and Manet traveled to the Netherlands for the second time. The poet Stéphane Mallarmé, who met the artist in 1873, wrote articles about him in 1874 and 1876 and remained a close lifelong friend. Manet declined to show with the Impressionists in their first exhibition in 1874. That summer he worked at Gennevilliers and Argenteuil with Monet and the following year he visited Venice. In 1876 at his own studio he exhibited the *Olympia* and two paintings rejected that year by the Salon. From 1879 to 1882 Manet participated annually at the Salon. He was given a one-man exhibition at Georges Charpentier's new gallery La Vie Moderne in Paris in 1880. The following year Manet, then ailing, was decorated by the Légion d'Honneur. He died in Paris on April 30, 1883; a memorial exhibition of his work took place at the Ecole des Beaux-Arts the following year.

2. BEFORE THE MIRROR. 1876
(Devant la glace)
Oil on canvas, 36¼ × 28⅛ in. (92.1 × 71.4 cm.)
Gift, Justin K. Thannhauser, 1978

In the late 1870s Manet executed several half-length studies of women dressing or bathing. The theme of a woman before a mirror appears also in his painting *Nana* (Collection Kunsthalle, Hamburg). In the example illustrated here the model, whose face and identity remain unknown, is shown with her back to the viewer: her blond hair, pinkish skin, and blue corset are rendered with expressive, fluid brushstrokes that dominate the canvas. Within the mirror, one does not find the woman's reflection but only strokes of paint. Manet's brushwork unites the picture surface, blurring distinctions of space and modeling and giving uniformity to foreground and background. Manet has ''set down'' the figure in paint with great freedom of handling and boldness in certain passages. As in other Impressionist paintings, no attempt has been made to finish the painting in a traditional sense.

E DGAR D EGAS 1834–1917. Hilaire-Germain-Edgar De Gas was born in Paris on July 19, 1834. Following his family's wishes, he began to study law but abandoned that pursuit in 1855 to become an artist. Starting in 1853, he copied often at the Louvre. As preparation for entrance into the Ecole des Beaux-Arts, he studied under Louis Lamothe, a former pupil of J.-A.-D. Ingres. In 1855 he was admitted to the Ecole but remained there only briefly. Degas spent 1856–57 in Florence, Rome, and Naples copying works by Italian masters, especially the Primitives. Throughout his life he continued to travel extensively, most frequently to Italy, but also to England, Spain, and the United States.

Starting in the early 1860s, Degas began to depict contemporary subjects: at first horses and racing scenes, later musicians, the opera, dancers, and circuses. From 1865 to 1870 he exhibited regularly at the Paris Salon, showing portraits for the most part. With the outbreak of the Franco-Prussian War in 1870, Degas enlisted in the infantry and was found to be almost blind in his right eye. His close friendship with Henri Rouart dates from 1870. Two years later he was introduced to Paul Durand-Ruel. In 1874 Degas's work was included in the first exhibition of the Impressionists; he showed in all but one of the seven subsequent exhibitions and helped organize several of them. Degas met Mary Cassatt about 1877, the year he invited her to join the Impressionist group. In the late 1870s he began to work seriously in sculpture, choosing as his subjects women bathing, horses, and dancers. His work was exhibited in London and New York in 1883, and Durand-Ruel showed him in New York in 1886. Degas met Gauguin in 1885. About 1890 Degas's eyesight began to fail. That same year he started to collect art intensively and eventually formed an impressive collection that included works by El Greco, Manet, Delacroix, and Gauguin as well as Japanese art. Degas's last one-man exhibition in his lifetime, comprising landscape pastels, was organized by Durand-Ruel in 1892. The artist died in Paris on or about September 26, 1917.

3. DANCERS IN GREEN AND YELLOW. c. 1903
(Danseuses vertes et jaunes)
Pastel on several pieces of paper mounted on board,
38⅞ × 28⅛ in. (98.8 × 71.5 cm.)
Gift, Justin K. Thannhauser, 1978

Throughout his long career Degas loved the world of ballet, theater, and music: he made this world and often—more specifically—the figures in it the subject of his art. *Dancers in Green and Yellow* is one of several very similar representations of a group of four dancers waiting in the wings that Degas executed about 1903. It was his practice to work in series, slightly modifying the same composition, repeating and refining the poses, and changing the color schemes. Degas's pastels first appeared in the mid-1870s and over the decades his compositions in this medium became bolder and his technique increasingly experimental. In *Dancers in Green and Yellow,* the artist has used pastel not so much to draw as to paint, applying layer upon layer of brilliant color. He has adjusted the proportions by adding strips of paper at the top and bottom. After his eyesight began to deteriorate, Degas concentrated increasingly on modeling figures of dancers and bathers; these were executed primarily between 1896 and 1911.

PIERRE-AUGUSTE RENOIR

1841–1919. Pierre-Auguste Renoir was born on February 25, 1841, in Limoges, and grew up in Paris. He worked as a commercial artist for several years and copied at the Louvre before entering the Ecole des Beaux-Arts in 1862 to study for one year with Emile Signol and Charles Gleyre. At Gleyre's private studio he met Monet, Frédéric Bazille, and Alfred Sisley, who joined him in plein-air painting.

In 1864 Renoir's first submission to the official Salon was accepted, and he began executing portrait commissions. The following year he visited the village of Marlotte near the forest of Fontainebleau for the first of many summers, and met Gustave Courbet. His work was accepted intermittently at the Salon until the early 1870s. In 1869 Renoir met Edmond Duranty, Paul Alexis, Zola, Cézanne, and the photographer Nadar (Félix Tournachon), and often painted with Monet. After army service during the Franco-Prussian War, he returned to Paris in 1871. In 1872 Renoir met the dealer Durand-Ruel and visited Gustave Caillebotte with Monet. He participated in the Salon des Refusés in 1873 and in the first exhibition of the group later known as the Impressionists in 1874. He took part in the second, third, and seventh Impressionist shows of 1876, 1877, and 1882, but declined to show in the other four. Financial difficulties forced Renoir and other Impressionists to organize an auction of their work at the Hôtel Drouot in 1875.

During the late 1870s Renoir associated with Guillaumin, Jules Champfleury, Cézanne, and the paint dealer Père Tanguy. From 1878 to 1883 he showed annually at the Salon. He visited Algeria and Italy in 1881 and returned to Algeria in 1882. In 1883 Durand-Ruel gave him a one-man show, and the artist traveled to the islands of Jersey and Guernsey and to L'Estaque to see Cézanne. Renoir exhibited with the group Les XX in Brussels in 1885, 1886, and 1889. He began a lifelong association with Stéphane Mallarmé in 1887. That same year he showed his *Bathers* at the Exposition Internationale in Paris. In 1890 he participated in the Salon for the last time, and was awarded the medal of the Légion d'Honneur. Despite failing health Renoir continued to work until his death at Cagnes on December 3, 1919.

4. WOMAN WITH PARROT. 1871
(La Femme au perroquet)
Oil on canvas, 36¼ × 25⅝ in. (92.1 × 65.1 cm.)
Gift, Justin K. Thannhauser, 1978

The woman holding the parrot is Renoir's friend Lise Tréhot (1848–1922), whose pretty, youthful features are recognizable in other canvases the artist painted between 1867 and 1872. He probably executed this picture soon after his return from service in the Franco-Prussian War in March 1871 and certainly before Lise married someone else in April 1872, evidently never to see Renoir again. The black silk dress with white cuffs and red sash accentuate Lise's dark hair and white skin; the dark green walls and plants suggest a rather heavy and formal interior decorated in the Second Empire style.

The subject of a woman holding a parrot appears in works from the 1860s by Courbet, Manet, and Degas. The formal, static composition and the representation of spatial depth and traditional modeling in Renoir's painting are consistent with his pictures from the late sixties and early seventies. *Woman with Parrot* clearly predates Renoir's Impressionist style and does not yet reflect the high-keyed tonality, shimmering patterns of light, and spontaneity of mood that would characterize his later work.

GEORGES SEURAT

1859–1891. Georges-Pierre Seurat was born on December 2, 1859, in Paris, which was to remain his home throughout his life. In 1878 he began studying with Henri Lehmann, a pupil of Ingres, at the Ecole des Beaux-Arts. About this time Seurat became interested in the work of Puvis de Chavannes and encountered Impressionist painting. He studied the color theories of Michel-Eugène Chevreul, Charles Blanc, David Sutter, Ogden N. Rood, and others. In 1879 he completed military service in Brest, returning to Paris the following year. During the early 1880s Seurat's work was influenced by Corot, Jean-François Millet, and the Barbizon painters; he also admired the paintings of Delacroix. In 1883 he began his first important oil, *Une Baignade, Asnières*, and participated in the official Paris Salon. The following year he was one of the founders of the Société des Artistes Indépendants; he remained active in its affairs until his death. Seurat and Signac became acquainted at meetings of the society and soon emerged as leaders of the Neo-Impressionists.

In 1885 Seurat met Pissarro, who invited him to participate in the eighth and final Impressionist exhibition, held in 1886. He showed *A Sunday Afternoon on the Island of La Grande Jatte* in this exhibition and again in the Indépendants exhibition of the same year. *Une Baignade* was shown by Durand-Ruel in New York in 1886, the year that also marks the beginning of Seurat's friendship with Félix Fénéon. From 1886 until his death Seurat exhibited annually with the Indépendants; he participated in shows of the group Les XX in Brussels in 1886, 1887, 1889, and 1891. In 1887 and 1888 he contributed drawings to the weekly *La Vie moderne*. During the last years of his life, the artist summered in Channel coast towns such as Honfleur, Port-en-Bassin, Le Crotoy, and Gravelines. Seurat died in Paris on March 29, 1891, at the age of thirty-one. Memorial exhibitions of his work were held in 1892 by Les XX in Brussels and the Indépendants in Paris.

5. SEATED WOMAN. 1883

(Femme assise)
Oil on canvas, 15 × 18 in. (38.1 × 46.2 cm.)
Gift, Solomon R. Guggenheim, 1937

Early in the 1880s Seurat investigated the color theories of Blanc, Chevreul, and Rood; he explored the ways their theories could be incorporated into his pictures by breaking down different hues and systematically applying small dabs of paint to his canvases. In paintings such as *Seated Woman* the artist's handling of color contrasts and his use of "divided" rather than mixed color reveal an understanding of Rood's theories. The woman's dress, which is blue-violet, contains touches of the opposites of these colors, namely orange and yellow; likewise, there are orange and purple strokes of pigment on her face.

Seated Woman, which was painted in 1883, presents the figure in a strongly silhouetted profile view against a field. Seurat has omitted any indication of a horizon line or sky and has depicted the field with "broom-swept" brushstrokes—colored strokes of meticulously applied dabs of pigment that create a dominant and unified surface pattern. The composition as well as the palette and brushwork demonstrate Pissarro's influence. In 1885 Seurat met the elder painter and Seurat's innovative use of finely divided brushstrokes was subsequently adopted by Pissarro: a significant case of reciprocal influences.

PAUL CÉZANNE

1839–1906. Paul Cézanne was born on January 19, 1839, in Aix-en-Provence. In 1854 he enrolled in the free drawing academy there, which he attended intermittently for several years. In 1858 he graduated from the Collège Bourbon, where he had become an intimate friend of his fellow student Zola. Cézanne entered the law school of the University of Aix in 1859 to placate his father, but abandoned his studies to join Zola in Paris in 1861. For the next twenty years Cézanne divided his time between the Midi and Paris. In the capital he briefly attended the Académie Suisse with Pissarro, who later became an important influence on his art. In 1862 Cézanne began long friendships with Monet and Renoir. His paintings were included in the 1863 Salon des Refusés. The Salon itself rejected Cézanne's submissions each year from 1864 to 1869.

In 1870, following the declaration of the Franco-Prussian War, Cézanne left Paris for Aix and then nearby L'Estaque, where he continued to paint. He made the first of several visits to Pontoise in 1872; there he worked alongside Pissarro. He participated in the first Impressionist exhibition of 1874. From 1876 to 1879 his works were again consistently rejected at the Salon. He showed again with the Impressionists in 1877 in their third exhibition. At this time Georges Rivière was one of the few critics to support Cézanne's art. In 1882 the Salon accepted his work for the first and only time. From 1883 Cézanne resided in the south of France, although he returned to Paris occasionally.

In 1890 he exhibited with the group Les XX in Brussels and spent five months in Switzerland. He traveled to Giverny in 1894 to visit Monet, who introduced him to Auguste Rodin and the critic Gustave Geffroy. Cézanne's first one-man show was held at Ambroise Vollard's gallery in Paris in 1895. From that point on he received increasing recognition. In 1899 he participated in the Salon des Indépendants in Paris for the first time. The following year he took part in the Centennial Exhibition in Paris. In 1903 the Berlin and Vienna Secessions included Cézanne's work, and in 1904 he exhibited at the Salon d'Automne, Paris. That same year he was given a solo exhibition at the Galerie Cassirer in Berlin. Cézanne died on October 22, 1906, in Aix-en-Provence.

6. MAN WITH CROSSED ARMS. c. 1899
(Homme aux bras croisés)
Oil on canvas, 36¼ × 28⅝ in. (92 × 72.7 cm.)
Acquired 1954

A late portrait like *Man with Crossed Arms* follows Cézanne's paintings of *Cardplayers* and *Smokers* from earlier in the 1890s in his selection of a model whose anonymity is preserved. Thus, the artist concentrates upon the massive shape of the sitter as it dominates the canvas, the acuteness and restlessness of his upward gaze, the simplification of volumes into planes, and the realization of the whole through subdued, close-valued brushstrokes. When this painting is compared with another version of *Man with Crossed Arms* (Collection Mrs. Carleton Mitchell, Annapolis, Maryland), subtle details unique to the Guggenheim's canvas, such as the way Cézanne presents the head at an angle, slants the shoulders, broadens the span of the crossed arms, emphasizes the discontinuity of the molding behind the sitter, and includes a stretcher and a palette flat upon the picture plane at the lower left, are immediately apparent. Cézanne endows the figure with a presence that is not only physical but psychological and spiritual.

VINCENT VAN GOGH

1853–1890. Vincent Willem van Gogh was born on March 30, 1853, in Groot-Zundert, the Netherlands. Starting in 1896, he worked for a firm of art dealers and at various short-lived jobs. By 1877 Van Gogh began religious studies and from 1878 to 1880 he was an evangelist in the Borinage, a poor mining district in Belgium. While working as an evangelist, he decided to become an artist. Vincent admired Millet and Honoré Daumier, and his early subjects were primarily peasants depicted in dark colors. He lived in Brussels and in various parts of the Netherlands before moving to Paris in February 1886.

In Paris he lived with his brother Theo and encountered Impressionist and Post-Impressionist painting. Van Gogh worked briefly at Fernand Cormon's atelier, where he met Henri de Toulouse-Lautrec. The artist also met Emile Bernard, Signac, Degas, Pissarro, and Gauguin at this time. Flowers, portraits, and scenes of Montmartre as well as a brighter palette replaced his earlier subject matter and tonalities. Van Gogh often worked in Asnières with Bernard and Signac in 1887.

In February of the following year, Van Gogh moved to Arles, where he painted in isolation, depicting the Provençal landscape and people. Gauguin joined him in the autumn, and the two artists worked together. Vincent suffered his first mental breakdown in December of 1888; numerous seizures and intermittent confinements in mental hospitals in Arles, Saint-Rémy, and Auvers-sur-Oise followed from that time until 1890. Nevertheless, he continued to paint. In 1890 Van Gogh was invited to show with Les XX in Brussels, where he sold his first painting. That same year he was represented at the Salon des Indépendants in Paris. Van Gogh shot himself at Auvers on July 27, 1890, and died on July 29.

7. MOUNTAINS AT SAINT-RÉMY. July 1889
(*Montagnes à Saint-Rémy*)
Oil on canvas, 28¼ × 35¾ in. (71.8 × 90.8 cm.)
Gift, Justin K. Thannhauser, 1978

In *Mountains at Saint-Rémy* Van Gogh depicts the Alpilles, a low, rugged mountain range visible from the hospital of Saint-Paul-de-Mausole in Saint-Rémy, where he was a patient in 1889. He has emphasized the undulating and contorted line of the mountain peaks by repeating patterns of brushstrokes that delineate the slopes. The upper portion of the canvas displays heavily brushed blue pigment that functions as a visual equivalent for the sky and echoes the curvilinear shapes in the lower half. Van Gogh's powerful, thick strokes not only give contour and form but also provide directional movement and expressive energy. The intensity of Van Gogh's painting derives primarily from the forms with their tumultuous, convoluted contours rather than from the colors. In this and other Saint-Rémy landscapes his colors, while still bold, have become noticeably more restrained than in previous years.

About July 9, 1889, Van Gogh mentioned *Mountains at Saint-Rémy* in a letter to his brother Theo: "The last canvas I have done is a view of mountains with a dark hut at the bottom among some olive trees." A month later he referred to the painting again and associated it with a passage in a book he was reading, Edouard Rod's *Le Sens de la vie*, describing "a desolate country of somber mountains, among which are some dark goatherds' huts where sunflowers are blooming."

Paul Gauguin

PAUL GAUGUIN 1848–1903. Paul Gauguin was born on June 7, 1848, in Paris and lived in Lima, Peru, from 1851 to 1855. He served in the merchant marine from 1865 to 1871 and traveled in the tropics. Gauguin later worked as a stockbroker's clerk in Paris but painted in his free time: he began working with Pissarro in 1874 and showed in every Impressionist exhibition between 1879 and 1886. By 1884 Gauguin had moved with his family to Copenhagen, where he unsuccessfully pursued a business career. He returned to Paris in 1885 to paint full time, leaving his family in Denmark.

In 1885 Gauguin met Degas; the next year he met Charles Laval and Bernard in Pont-Aven and Van Gogh in Paris. With Laval he traveled to Panama and Martinique in 1887 in search of more exotic subject matter. Increasingly, Gauguin turned to primitive cultures for inspiration. In Brittany again in 1888 he met Paul Sérusier and renewed his acquaintanceship with Bernard. As self-designated Synthetists, they were welcomed in Paris by the Symbolist literary and artistic circle. Gauguin organized a group exhibition of their work at the Café Volpini, Paris, in 1889, in conjunction with the World's Fair in that city. In 1891 Gauguin auctioned his paintings to raise money for a voyage to Tahiti, which he undertook that same year.

In 1893 illness forced him to return to Paris, where, with the critic Charles Morice, he began *Noa Noa*, a book about Tahiti. Gauguin was able to return to Tahiti in 1895. He unsuccessfully attempted suicide in January 1898, not long after completing his mural-sized painting *D'où venons nous? Qui sommes nous? Où allons nous?* In 1899 he championed the cause of French settlers in Tahiti in a political journal, *Les Guêpes*, and founded his own periodical, *Le Sourire*. Gauguin's other writings, which were autobiographical, include *Cahier pour Aline* (1892), *L'Esprit moderne et le catholicisme* (1897 and 1902), and *Avant et après* (1902). In 1901, the artist moved to the Marquesas, where he died on May 8, 1903. A major retrospective of his works was held at the Salon d'Automne in Paris in 1906.

8. IN THE VANILLA GROVE, MAN AND HORSE. 1891

(*Dans la vanillière, homme et cheval*)
Oil on burlap, 28¾ × 36¼ in. (73 × 92 cm.)
Gift, Justin K. Thannhauser, 1978

Gauguin first traveled to Tahiti in 1891: he arrived there in early June and probably began to paint in September. At least twenty canvases date from the autumn of 1891 and many portray the artist's new surroundings in this Tahitian landscape. *In the Vanilla Grove, Man and Horse* shows two large foreground figures juxtaposed with dense foliage, which conceals two female figures who appear to be tending vanilla plants. Gauguin contrasts the man and horse in the foreground with the stylized landscape in the background. Man and horse are presented in close proximity; their boldly outlined forms are derived from a similar pair that appears on the West Frieze of the Parthenon. Gauguin turned to Greek, Egyptian, Indian, Javanese, and Primitive art for images and he is known to have used photographs for specific motifs. In this painting both the abstract color areas in the foreground and the tapestry-like foliage in the background compress space. Flat, colored shapes can be perceived as surface patterns. Like Van Gogh, Gauguin sought bright light, which tends to flatten volumes into areas of intense color.

HENRI DE TOULOUSE-LAUTREC

1864–1901. Henri-Marie-Raymond de Toulouse-Lautrec-Monfa was born in 1864 at Albi of an aristocratic family. Two childhood accidents, which stunted the growth of his legs, left him permanently dwarfed. He began to paint during his adolescence, encouraged by the animal painter René Princeteau, a family friend. With the financial support of his family, he moved to Paris in 1881, and the following year began studying with Léon Bonnat. When Bonnat's studio closed in 1883, Toulouse-Lautrec worked in Fernand Cormon's atelier. He completed his studies in 1884 but remained in touch with members of this atelier, meeting Van Gogh in 1886 through Cormon's circle. Toulouse-Lautrec moved to Montmartre in 1884 and began what was to be a lifelong study of the inhabitants of Parisian music halls, cabarets, and brothels.

Toulouse-Lautrec's early style was strongly influenced by Impressionism. By the late 1880s, however, the artist had evolved a typically Art Nouveau style, his work increasingly characterized by large, flat areas of color and energetic outlines and reflecting the influences of both Degas and Japanese prints. In 1888 he exhibited for the first time at Les XX in Brussels and the following year he began showing annually with the Indépendants in Paris. He showed regularly in major exhibitions in the 1890s, and achieved popular acclaim during this period through his posters. The dance hall Le Moulin Rouge commissioned Toulouse-Lautrec's first lithographic poster in 1891, and thereafter the artist worked intensively in lithography, experimenting with the medium and producing many prints and posters. Toulouse-Lautrec experienced a mental and physical breakdown in 1899, and died on September 9, 1901, at his family's estate in the Gironde. He was thirty-seven years old.

9. AU SALON. 1893

Pastel, gouache, and pencil on cardboard, 20⅞ × 31⅜ in. (53 × 79.7 cm.)
Gift, Justin K. Thannhauser, 1978

Toulouse-Lautrec's work belongs to the Art Nouveau style, especially evident in the bold, decorative stylization of his posters and the synthesis of line and color in his lithographs. He favored the Parisian world of the theater, dance hall, brothel, café, and circus. In 1892 he painted decorations for a bordello in the rue d'Ambroise; for a while in 1894 he even lived in the most famous and luxurious whorehouse in the rue de Moulins. *Au Salon* is one of the many studies of brothel life that he did between 1892 and 1895. It reveals the artist's acute observation of detail and his penchant for choosing scenes from the daily routine as subject matter for his art. Through the attitudes of the three women and the discordant, rather oppressive colors, Toulouse-Lautrec projects an atmosphere heavy with boredom.

LIBRARY
UNIVERSITY OF ST. FRANCIS
JOLIET, ILLINOIS

Henri Rousseau

1844–1910. Born on May 21, 1844, in Laval, France, Henri-Julien-Félix Rousseau attended the lycée there until 1860. While working for a lawyer in 1863, Rousseau was charged with petty larceny and joined the army to avoid scandal. He never saw combat and did not travel outside of France, but his colleagues' adventures in Mexico inspired him to create legends of his own foreign journeys. Upon his father's death in 1868, Rousseau left the army. The following year he entered the Paris municipal toll-collecting service as a second-class clerk; he was never promoted although he has traditionally been called "Le Douanier" (customs official). In 1884 Rousseau obtained a permit to sketch in the national museums. He sent two paintings to the Salon des Champs-Elysées in 1885 and from 1886 until his death he exhibited annually at the Salon des Indépendants.

By 1893 Rousseau retired from the Paris toll service on a small pension and began to paint full time. That same year he met the writer Alfred Jarry, who encouraged him and introduced him into literary circles. In 1899 the artist wrote a five-act play entitled *La Vengeance d'une orpheline russe (A Russian Orphan's Revenge)*. A waltz he composed, "Clémence," was published in 1904. Rousseau had become friendly with Robert Delaunay by 1906. The year 1908 saw the beginning of the musical and family evenings Rousseau held in his studio in the rue Perrel. Late that year Pablo Picasso arranged a banquet in honor of Rousseau which Marie Laurencin, the writers Guillaume Apollinaire and Max Jacob, and others attended.

By 1909 Rousseau's paintings were being acquired by the dealers Ambroise Vollard and Joseph Brummer. His first one-man show was arranged in 1909 by Wilhelm Uhde and took place in a furniture shop in the rue Notre-Dame-des-Champs. Rousseau died on September 2, 1910, in Paris. That same year an exhibition of his work, culled from the collection of Max Weber, took place at Alfred Stieglitz's gallery "291" in New York. He was given a retrospective at the Salon des Indépendants in 1911.

10. The Football Players. 1908
(Les Joueurs de football)
Oil on canvas, 39½ × 31⅝ in. (100.5 × 80.3 cm.)
Acquired 1960

The Football Players is the artist's attempt to depict a group of athletes in motion, a rare work among Rousseau's basically static paintings. The tree trunks, symmetrically placed at each side of the composition, mark spatial recession, and the horizontal division of the canvas creates a perspectival framework. As Daniel Catton Rich observed, there is something ballet-like in the stylized poses of the football players. The athletes with their striped attire are shown in pairs, and the stiffness of their gestures is echoed by the four trees in the background.

Rousseau painted *The Football Players* with surprisingly light, high-keyed color and rendered the foliage with meticulous attention to detail. The artist used to walk from Paris out to the suburban countryside to sketch but would finish his work in the studio. In this carefully worked picture, figures and landscape combine to form an otherworldly environment.

EDOUARD VUILLARD

1868–1940. Edouard Vuillard was born on November 11, 1868, in Cuiseaux, France. In 1878 his family moved to Paris and Edouard attended the Lycée Condorcet. There he met his future brother-in-law, K.-X. Roussel, as well as Maurice Denis and A.-F. Lugné-Poë, who was to become a leading theater director. In 1888 Vuillard and Roussel attended the Académie Julian, where they joined forces with the artists who would soon call themselves Nabis: Sérusier, Paul Ranson, Denis, and Pierre Bonnard. "Nabi" is the Hebrew word for prophet; the Nabis, influenced by Gauguin and Japanese prints, experimented with arbitrary color, expressive line, and flat, patterned surfaces. They sought practical application for their art beyond easel painting to realms such as stage design and architectural decoration. Vuillard began exhibiting with them in 1891 at Le Barc de Boutteville.

In the early years of his career he designed theatrical sets and programs, posters, and illustrations. Ambroise Vollard commissioned him to do an album of color lithographs in 1896. The Natanson brothers, founders of the avant-garde periodical *La Revue blanche,* and Mme Hessel, director of Galerie Bernheim-Jeune, were Vuillard's close friends and important patrons. He accepted commissions to decorate homes and public buildings: the decorations completed in 1913 for the foyer of the newly built Comédie des Champs-Elysées are still in existence. Vuillard exhibited often at the Salon des Indépendants until 1910 and at the Salon d'Automne until 1912. After that and until the late 1930s, his work was rarely shown, except at Bernheim-Jeune, where he exhibited regularly. He executed many paintings of his mother and the interior of the apartment they shared until her death in 1928. The artist continued to live quietly in Paris until the end of his life.

In the late thirties he did decorations for the League of Nations, Geneva, and for the Palais de Chaillot, Paris. In 1938 he was given a major retrospective at the Musée des Arts Décoratifs in Paris. Vuillard died on June 21, 1940, in La Baule.

11. PLACE VINTIMILLE. 1908–10

Distemper on cardboard mounted on canvas, two panels, 78¾ × 27⅜ in. (200 × 69.5 cm.); 78¾ × 27½ in. (200 × 69.9 cm.)
Gift, Justin K. Thannhauser, 1978

The two panels of *Place Vintimille* were part of a series of eight that Vuillard painted for the playwright Henry Bernstein, who had them installed in his home in Paris. Place Vintimille (now place Adolf Max) was a recurrent subject in Vuillard's work after 1907, when he lived in a fourth-floor apartment overlooking the square. Like Bonnard, Vuillard closely observed details of life around him: horse-drawn carriages, dogs, children playing, the chill gray light of Paris, and the bare branches of trees.

The origins of the technique employed by Vuillard in *Place Vintimille* can be traced to his early years of painting when he used cardboard and distemper for reasons of economy. He continued to paint with this medium, familiar from set designs, as he favored the absorbency of the support and the resultant matt tonality.

Pierre Bonnard

PIERRE BONNARD 1867–1947. Pierre Bonnard was born on October 3, 1867, at Fontenay-aux-Roses, France. He began law studies in Paris in 1887. That same year Bonnard also attended the Académie Julian and in 1888 entered the Ecole des Beaux-Arts, where he met K.-X. Roussel and Vuillard, both of whom became his lifelong friends. Thus, Bonnard gave up law to become an artist, and, after brief military service, in 1889 he joined the group of young painters called the Nabis.

In 1890 Bonnard shared a studio with Vuillard and Denis, and he began to make color lithographs. The following year he met Toulouse-Lautrec. Also in 1891 he showed for the first time at the Salon des Indépendants and in the Nabis' earliest exhibitions at Le Barc de Boutteville. Bonnard exhibited with the Nabis until they disbanded in 1900. He worked in a variety of mediums; for example, he frequently made posters and illustrations for *La Revue blanche* and in 1895 he designed a stained-glass window for Louis Comfort Tiffany. His first one-man show, at the Galerie Durand-Ruel in 1896, included paintings, posters, and lithographs; in 1897 Ambroise Vollard published the first of many albums of Bonnard's lithographs and illustrated books.

In 1903 Bonnard participated in the first Salon d'Automne and in the Vienna Secession; as of 1906 he was represented by Galerie Bernheim-Jeune. He traveled abroad extensively and worked at various locations in Normandy, the Seine valley, and the south of France (he bought a villa at Le Cannet near Cannes in 1925) as well as in Paris. The Art Institute of Chicago mounted a major Bonnard-Vuillard exhibition in 1933, and The Museum of Modern Art, New York, organized Bonnard retrospectives in 1946 and 1964. Bonnard died at Le Cannet on January 23, 1947.

12. DINING ROOM ON THE GARDEN. 1934–35
(Grande salle à manger sur le jardin)
Oil on canvas, 50 × 53¼ in. (126.8 × 135.3 cm.)
Acquired 1938

Like his friend Vuillard, Bonnard preferred to paint familiar interior scenes, landscapes, and decorative panels. The Guggenheim's painting represents the dining room in the villa Bonnard rented only for the summer of 1934 at Bénerville-sur-Mer near Deauville on the Channel coast.

The theme of a still life in front of a window had appeared frequently in the work of Henri Matisse and Picasso. Yet *Dining Room on the Garden* reflects Bonnard's individuality as a painter: in the glowing colors and distinctive value contrasts, in the dominance of the picture plane, and in the figure of the artist's wife, Marthe, whose presence is so often felt in his pictures. A very similar painting, *Table Before Window* (Collection Edward A. Bragaline, New York), contains a still life, the flattened pattern of a chair in front of the window, and Bonnard's wife at the right. In these canvases the windows vertically structure an otherwise indeterminate space. They also provide a visually logical transition between the warm-toned intimacy of the interior and the cool blues outside.

ARISTIDE MAILLOL

1861–1944. Aristide-Joseph-Bonaventure Maillol was born on December 9, 1861, in Banyuls-sur-Mer, France. He went to Paris in 1882 to study painting and in 1885 was admitted to the Ecole des Beaux-Arts, where he studied with Jean-Léon Gérôme and Alexandre Cabanel. He became dissatisfied with his academic training in 1889, partly due to his discovery of Gauguin's paintings, pottery, and wood carving. During the 1890s he concentrated on making tapestries, ceramics, and decorative wood carvings, in response to the Arts and Crafts movement popular in France at the time. In 1896 he showed small carved figures for the first time, at the Salon de la Société Nationale des Beaux-Arts. Maillol became friends with Denis, Bonnard, Vuillard, and the rest of the Nabis during the mid-nineties.

By 1900 deteriorating eyesight forced him to give up tapestry and concentrate on sculpture. Maillol's first one-man exhibition was held at the Galerie Vollard in Paris in 1902. In 1905 his first monumental sculpture, *The Mediterranean,* was shown at the Salon d'Automne, Paris, prompting the German Count Harry Kessler to commission a version in stone (the original was in bronze). That same year Maillol was commissioned to execute *Action in Chains,* a memorial to Louis-Auguste Blanqui, for the town of Puget-Théniers. In 1907 he completed the relief *Desire* and a statue, the *Young Cyclist,* for his patron Kessler.

In 1910 Maillol began a monument to Cézanne that was finally installed in the Tuileries Gardens of Paris in 1929. From 1919 to 1923 he worked on two war memorials for the towns of Céret and Port-Vendres. His first one-man show in the United States took place at the Albright Art Gallery in Buffalo in 1925. In 1930 he received a commission for a war memorial from the town of Banyuls and another for a monument to Claude Debussy in Saint-Germain-en-Laye. Major Maillol retrospectives were held at the Galerie Flechtheim, Berlin, 1928, and the Kunsthalle Basel in 1933. In 1938 he began his last monument commissions, a memorial to aviators entitled *Air,* for the city of Toulouse, and one called *The River,* in memory of Henri Barbusse. Maillol died on September 27, 1944, in Banyuls.

13. POMONA WITH LOWERED ARMS. Late 1920s
(Pomone aux bras tombants)
Bronze, 65¾ in. (167 cm.) high
Acquired 1958

Maillol demonstrated a preference for representing the female figure. The composition and pose of *Pomona with Lowered Arms* ultimately derive from Greek art but the voluptuous figure type is that of the women of his native Banyuls. During his lifetime Maillol executed many versions of Pomona. The earliest was a plaster of *Pomona with Raised Arms,* which was exhibited at the Salon d'Automne in Paris in 1910; the pose later was used in *The Seasons.* A related draped figure became a World War I memorial at Elne. By the late 1920s Maillol altered the position of the arms in a plaster from which this cast was made. A marble of Pomona with lowered arms holding apples dates from 1937 (Collection Musée du Petit Palais, Paris).

It was Maillol's practice to return to themes and compositions he had treated earlier. Thus, the sculptures from the 1930s are often new versions of works originally executed during the first decade of the twentieth century.

EDVARD MUNCH

1863–1944. Edvard Munch was born on December 12, 1863, in Løten, Norway. In 1864 his family moved to Oslo (then Christiania), where both his mother and sister died while he was young. He abandoned engineering studies to dedicate himself to painting in 1880. Munch enrolled in the Royal School of Design in Oslo in 1881 and exhibited for the first time in the Autumn Salon of Oslo in 1883. During these years he associated with a circle of advanced Norwegian artists and writers. In 1884 he attended an open-air academy in Modum directed by Frits Thaulow.

On a scholarship Thaulow awarded him in 1885, Munch traveled to Paris. That same year he began *The Morning After, Puberty,* and *The Sick Child. The Sick Child* created a scandal at Oslo's Autumn Salon of 1886. In 1889, the year of his first one-man show in Oslo, Munch received the first of three state scholarships and went again to Paris, where he entered Léon Bonnat's new art school. As early as 1891 he painted works that would later be included in his *Frieze of Life,* a monumental series of paintings about love and death. His show at the Verein Berliner Künstler in Berlin in 1892 was closed after a week of heated debate. While living in Berlin from 1892 to 1895, Munch produced his first etchings and lithographs and frequented the literary and artistic group that was connected with the periodical *Pan* and included August Strindberg and Julius Meier-Graefe. He took part in the Salon des Indépendants in Paris in 1897 and visited Italy two years later. He joined the Société des Artistes Indépendants in Paris in 1903 and the Secession group in Berlin in 1904.

In 1908 the Nasjonalgalleriet, Oslo, purchased a number of Munch's works. That autumn he suffered a nervous breakdown and entered a clinic in Copenhagen, where he remained for several months. From 1909 to 1914 Munch worked on the *Aula* murals for the Oslo University Assembly Hall; in 1913 his prints were included in the Armory Show in New York. Three years later he moved to Ekely at Skøyen, where he spent most of his remaining years. In his work Munch continued to explore such major themes as those expressed in *The Voice, Kiss, Madonna, Melancholy, The Sick Child,* and *Death in the Sickroom.* In 1922 the artist was given a major retrospective at the Kunsthaus Zürich; in 1927 comprehensive exhibitions of his work were held at the Nationalgalerie, Berlin, and the Nasjonalgalleriet, Oslo. Munch died in Skøyen on January 23, 1944; he left all of his work to the city of Oslo.

14. SKETCH OF THE MODEL POSING. 1893
Pastel on cardboard, 30⅛ × 20⅞ in.
(76.7 × 55.5 cm.)
Acquired 1970

The year 1893 was a remarkably productive and innovative time for Munch. For the most part he lived in Berlin and worked on a series of paintings for his *Frieze of Life* project. *Sketch of the Model Posing* is stylistically and chronologically related to this monumental series. In the Guggenheim's pastel, the woman's face is averted, her head tipped back at a distinctive angle, the curves of her body echoed and enclosed by linear patterns. This pastel is an evocative figure study that cannot be specifically related to a final work. Munch, who was fascinated with the stages of life, portrayed women as symbolic images: as the youthful Virgin, Madonna, Vampire, and as Old Age. The pictorial organization, the emphatic repetition of lines, and the stylized contours in this early work suggest the swirling, expressive shapes of Art Nouveau.

HENRI MATISSE

HENRI MATISSE 1869–1954. Henri-Emile-Benoît Matisse was born on December 31, 1869, in Le Cateau-Cambrésis, France. He grew up at Bohain-en-Vermandois and studied law in Paris from 1887 to 1889. By 1891 he had abandoned law and started to paint. In Paris Matisse studied art briefly at the Académie Julian and then at the Ecole des Beaux-Arts with Gustave Moreau.

In 1901 Matisse exhibited at the Salon des Indépandants in Paris and met the other future leaders of the Fauve movement, Maurice de Vlaminck and André Derain. His first one-man show took place at the Galerie Vollard in 1904. Both Leo and Gertrude Stein as well as Etta and Claribel Cone began to collect Matisse's work at this time. Like many avant-garde artists in Paris, Matisse was receptive to a broad range of influences; he was one of the first painters to take an interest in Primitive art. Matisse abandoned the palette of the Impressionists and established his characteristic style with its flat, brilliant color and fluid line. His subjects were mainly women, interiors, and still lifes. In 1913 his work was included in the Armory Show in New York. By 1923 two Russians, Sergei Shchukin and Ivan Morosov, had purchased nearly fifty of his paintings.

From the early twenties until 1939 Matisse divided his time primarily between the south of France and Paris. During this period he worked on painting, sculpture, lithographs, and etchings as well as on murals for The Barnes Foundation in Pennsylvania, designs for tapestries, and set and costume designs for Léonide Massine's ballet, *Rouge et noir (Red and Black)*. While recuperating from two major operations in 1941 and 1942, Matisse concentrated on a technique he had devised earlier, *papiers découpés* (paper cutouts). *Jazz*, written and illustrated by Matisse, was published in 1947. The plates are stencil reproductions of paper cutouts. In 1948 he began the design and decoration of the Chapelle du Rosaire at Vence, which was completed and consecrated in 1951. Matisse continued to make his large paper cutouts, the last of which was a design for the rose window at Union Church of Pocantico Hills, New York. He died in Nice on November 3, 1954.

15. THE ITALIAN WOMAN. Early 1916

(L'Italienne)
Oil on canvas, 46 × 35¼ in. (116.6 × 89.6 cm.)
Acquired by exchange, 1982

Matisse's painting *The Italian Woman*, which was completed in early 1916, conveys an extraordinarily vivid sense of the evolution of a work of art. The figure emerges from the flat canvas and presses against its vertical boundaries: the woman's head touches the top of the canvas and her tensely clasped hands are firmly anchored at the bottom edge. Her face is serious, austere, sculptural; her black hair hangs like a curtain to one side. The subject is Laurette, an Italian model who posed for Matisse from late 1915 until 1918 and whose features are recognizable in other paintings. A photograph of Matisse's studio shows an earlier stage of *The Italian Woman* and documents a more realistic portrayal of Laurette before the artist decided to rework the canvas. However, the changes, or pentimenti, are clearly visible in the present picture, especially in the model's right shoulder, face, and hair. Matisse has covered Laurette's right shoulder with the tan background and he has accentuated her left arm with a green pigment that ties it to the adjacent green background. He plays upon contrasts between left and right, foreground and background, and the three-dimensional figure and two-dimensional surface of the picture. *The Italian Woman* articulates the intensity of the figure and embodies the very process of making a picture.

GEORGES BRAQUE 1882–1963.

Georges Braque was born in Argenteuil-sur-Seine on May 13, 1882. He grew up in Le Havre and studied evenings at the Ecole des Beaux-Arts there from about 1897 to 1899. He left for Paris to study under a master decorator and received his craftsman certificate in 1901. From 1902 to 1904 he painted at the Académie Humbert in Paris, where he met Marie Laurencin and Francis Picabia. By 1906 Braque's work was no longer Impressionist but Fauve in style; after spending that summer in Antwerp with Othon Friesz, he showed his Fauve work the following year in the Salon des Indépendants in Paris. His first one-man show was at D.-H. Kahnweiler's gallery in 1908. Starting in 1909 Picasso and Braque worked together in developing Cubism; by 1911 their styles were extremely similar. In 1912 they started to incorporate collage elements into their painting and experiment with the *papier collé* (pasted paper) technique. Their artistic collaboration lasted until 1914. Braque was wounded during World War I; upon his recovery in 1917 he began a close friendship with Juan Gris.

After World War I his work became freer and less schematic. His fame grew in 1922 as a result of a major

16. LANDSCAPE NEAR ANTWERP. 1906
(Paysage près d'Anvers)
Oil on canvas, 23⅝ × 31⅞ in. (60 × 81 cm.)
Gift, Justin K. Thannhauser, 1978

The Fauve paintings by Matisse and Derain at the Salon d'Automne in Paris in the autumn of 1905 profoundly impressed Braque. The artist painted his first Fauve works during the summer of 1906, which he spent in Antwerp. The distant harbor on the Scheldt River, complete with masts of ships, is represented in *Landscape near Antwerp.*

Braque employed non-naturalistic color and stylized brushwork in his Fauve paintings: curving contour lines and strokes of contrasting pigment become the visual equivalent for the landscape. In this early Fauve picture the pale violet and green in the sky, the yellow and lavender in the water, and the expressive reds, oranges, and yellows create a vivid harmony that derives not from the actual landscape but from the imaginative world of the artist. Braque's colors became more extreme and his brushwork more abbreviated in the canvases he painted at L'Estaque in the south of France during the autumn of 1906 and into the winter of 1907. The artist's Fauve manner continued through 1907, but the following year marks the beginning of his Cubist style.

exhibition at the Salon d'Automne in Paris. In the mid-twenties Braque designed the decor for two Sergei Diaghilev ballets. By the end of the decade he had returned to a more realistic interpretation of nature, although certain aspects of Cubism always remained present in his work. In 1931 Braque made his first engraved plasters and began to portray mythological subjects. His first important retrospective took place in 1933 at the Kunsthalle Basel. He won First Prize at the Carnegie International in Pittsburgh in 1937.

During World War II Braque remained in Paris. His paintings at that time, primarily still lifes and interiors, became more somber. In addition to painting Braque also made lithographs, engravings, and sculpture. From the late 1940s onward he explored various recurring themes such as birds, ateliers, landscapes, and seascapes. In 1953 he designed stained-glass windows for the church of Varengeville. During the last few years of his life Braque's ill health prevented him from undertaking further large-scale commissions but he continued to paint and make lithographs and jewelry designs. He died in Paris on August 31, 1963.

17a. VIOLIN AND PALETTE. 1909–10
(Violon et palette)
Oil on canvas, 36⅛ × 16⅞ in. (91.7 × 42.8 cm.)
Acquired 1954

17b. PIANO AND MANDOLA. 1909–10
(Piano et mandore)
Oil on canvas, 36⅛ × 16⅞ in. (91.7 × 42.8 cm.)
Acquired 1954

The companion pictures *Violin and Palette* and *Piano and Mandola*, painted during the winter of 1909–10, are classic examples of the early phase of Cubism. In both canvases, the objects represented are readily identifiable although their shapes have been fragmented. Braque stated that this fragmentation permitted him "to establish a spatial element as well as a spatial movement." He also remarked that he chose to paint musical instruments not only because he was surrounded by them in his studio but because he was "working towards a tactile space . . . and musical instruments have the advantage of being animated by one's touch." (D. Vallier, "Braque la peinture et nous," *Cahiers d'Art,* XXIXᵉ année, Oct. 1954, p. 16.)

Both still lifes exist in rather shallow space, and the forms are rendered with neutral colors, predominantly greens and browns. By limiting the pictorial element through the use of a subdued palette, Braque and Picasso concentrated on a new conception of space, on the disintegration of objects into faceted planes, and on other essentially formal problems of Analytical Cubism.

18. GUITAR, GLASS, AND FRUIT DISH ON SIDEBOARD. *Early 1919*

(Guitare, verre, et compotier sur un buffet)
Oil on canvas, 31⅞ × 39½ in. (81 × 100.3 cm.)
Gift, Justin K. Thannhauser Foundation, by
exchange, 1981

When Braque resumed painting after World War I, he limited his artistic production almost exclusively to still lifes. As subject matter he favored musical instruments, which he sometimes placed next to fruit or newspaper and often presented on a sideboard or table.

Here, departing from the style of his earlier Cubist works, Braque uses broad, flat planes of color to articulate the objects and define the shallow space. *Guitar, Glass, and Fruit Dish on Sideboard* is characterized by a black background, adjacent tan areas contrasting with the red and green patterned tablecloth, and three light blue zones. The artist preserves the integrity and materiality of the objects; he boldly flattens their forms but does not fragment them. In his Synthetic Cubist still lifes, of which this is an example, Braque explores the coloristic possibilities of objects and patterns and emphasizes the spatial implications of uniting them on a single painted surface.

PABLO PICASSO

PABLO PICASSO 1881–1973. Pablo Ruiz Picasso was born on October 25, 1881, at Málaga in Andalucia, Spain. The son of an academic painter, José Ruiz Blanco, he began to draw at an early age. In 1895 the family moved to Barcelona, and Picasso studied there at La Lonja, the academy of fine arts. His association with the group at the café Els Quatre Gats in Barcelona from 1898 and his visit to Horta de Ebro of 1898–99 were crucial to his early artistic development. In 1900 Picasso's first exhibition took place in Barcelona, and that autumn he went to Paris for what would be the first of several stays during the early years of the century. Picasso settled in Paris in April 1904 and soon his circle of friends included Max Jacob, Apollinaire, Gertrude and Leo Stein as well as two dealers, Ambroise Vollard and Berthe Weill.

His style developed from the Blue Period (1901 to 1904) to the Rose Period (1905) to the pivotal work *Les Demoiselles d'Avignon* (1907) and the subsequent evolution of Cubism from 1909 to 1911. Picasso's collaboration on ballet and theatrical productions began in 1916. Soon thereafter his work was characterized by neoclassicism and a renewed interest in drawing and figural representation. In the 1920s the artist continued to live in Paris, travel frequently, and spend summers at the beach. From 1925 to the early 1930s Picasso was involved to a certain degree with the Surrealists and from the autumn of 1931 he was especially interested in making sculpture. With the large exhibitions at the Galerie Georges Petit in Paris and the Kunsthaus Zürich in 1932 and the publication of the first volume of Christian Zervos's catalogue raisonné that same year, Picasso's fame increased markedly.

By 1936 the Spanish Civil War had exerted a profound effect on Picasso, the expression of which culminated in his painting *Guernica* (1937). He was also deeply moved by World War II and stayed primarily in Paris during those years. From the late 1940s onward he lived in the south of France. Among the enormous number of Picasso exhibitions that have been held, those at The Museum of Modern Art in New York in 1939 and 1980 have been most significant. In 1961 the artist married Jacqueline Roque and they moved to Mougins. There Picasso continued his prolific work in painting, drawing, prints, ceramics, and sculpture until his death on April 8, 1973.

19. WOMAN IRONING. 1904
(La Repasseuse)
Oil on canvas, 45¾ × 28¾ in. (116.2 × 73 cm.)
Gift, Justin K. Thannhauser, 1978

After several earlier visits, Picasso went back to Paris in April 1904 and remained there until 1948. He first stayed in Montmartre at 13, rue Ravignan in the building called the "Bateau-Lavoir," where many artists, including Gris, once lived. The large, haunting picture from the Thannhauser collection of a woman ironing dates from this period. Daumier and Degas had treated the subject before, as had Picasso himself in 1901. The expressive pose in this painting of the frail woman pressing down on the iron undoubtedly derives from Degas's work.

Woman Ironing still retains some of the somber tonality of Picasso's Blue Period. Both the neutral colors and the tense, angular figure express poverty, loneliness, and suffering. Like Picasso's *Old Guitarist* (Collection The Art Institute of Chicago), which was painted in Barcelona in 1903, the woman ironing has one shoulder raised in a distorted pose, the head low-ered and turned to the side so that it is seen in profile. The model appears in several of Picasso's canvases of 1904 and has been identified as Margot, the daughter of Frédé, who owned the café Le Lapin Agile, which Picasso and his friends frequented.

20. *ACCORDIONIST. Summer 1911*
(L'Accordéoniste)
Oil on canvas, 51¼ × 35¼ in. (130.2 × 89.5 cm.)
Gift, Solomon R. Guggenheim, 1937

During the summer of 1911 Picasso and Braque worked closely together at Céret in the French Pyrenees. Picasso's *Accordionist* demonstrates how far he had moved in the direction of abstraction. The traditional relationship between figure and ground has been destroyed and replaced by a unified pictorial configuration. The extreme degree of fragmentation, the flat, shaded planes, nondescriptive regularized brushstrokes, monochromatic color, and shallow space are characteristics of Analytical Cubism.

Picasso's *Accordionist* bears strong similarities to Braque's *Man with a Guitar*, summer 1911 (Collection The Museum of Modern Art, New York). As Robert Rosenblum has observed, both paintings have scroll patterns at the lower left, discernible indications of the sitter's fingers, and vestiges of facial features. Picasso in particular favored figure painting and often chose to depict people playing musical instruments: the Guggenheim's *Accordionist*, *"Ma Jolie,"* winter 1911–12 (Collection The Museum of Modern Art, New York), and *The Aficionado*, summer 1912 (Collection Kunstmuseum Basel), are testimony to that fact. In these paintings there is a strong two-dimensional unity of surface, a sense of light emanating from the forms themselves, and an articulation of the canvas that is dictated by the inner structure rather than by the arbitrary edges of the support.

21. MANDOLIN AND GUITAR. 1924
(Mandoline et guitare)
Oil with sand on canvas, 55⅜ × 78⅞ in.
(140.6 × 200.4 cm.)
Acquired 1953

During the summers of 1924 and 1925 Picasso painted
at least nine large colorful still lifes with an essentially
similar motif: an arrangement of objects on a centrally
situated table in front of an open window. This theme
appeared for the first time in a group of drawings and
watercolors Picasso did at Saint-Raphaël in 1919 when
he first summered on the Côte d'Azur.

The Guggenheim's canvas is structured by means of
flat color areas and decorative patterns. Its pictorial organization also depends upon the curved contours of
the still-life arrangement and the linear division of the
floor and background wall. The bold, bright colors, the
lively patterns of the tablecloth, and the sky and clouds
glimpsed through the window contribute essentially to
the picture's vitality.

FERNAND LÉGER

FERNAND LÉGER 1881–1955. Fernand Léger was born on February 4, 1881, at Argentan in Normandy. After apprenticing with an architect in Caen from 1897 to 1899, Léger settled in Paris in 1900 and supported himself as an architectural draftsman. He was refused entrance to the Ecole des Beaux-Arts, but nevertheless attended classes there; he also studied at the Académie Julian. Léger's earliest known works, which date from 1905, were primarily influenced by Impressionism. The experience of seeing the Cézanne retrospective at the Salon d'Automne in 1907 and his contact with the early Cubism of Picasso and Braque had an extremely significant impact on the development of his personal style. In 1910 he exhibited with Braque and Picasso at D.-H. Kahnweiler's gallery, where he was given a one-man show in 1912. From 1911 to 1914 Léger's work became increasingly abstract, and it was at this time that he started to limit his palette to the primary colors and black and white.

Léger served in the military from 1914 to 1917. His "mechanical" period, in which figures and objects are characterized by tubular, machine-like forms, began in 1917. During the early 1920s he collaborated with the writer

22. THE SMOKERS. December 1911–
January 1912
(Les Fumeurs)
Oil on canvas, 57⅝ × 38⅜ in. (146.3 × 97.5 cm.)
Gift, Solomon R. Guggenheim, 1938

Léger's Cubist works reveal a closer affinity to Robert Delaunay's dynamic Cubism than to the static Cubism of Braque and Picasso. Like many of Delaunay's paintings of the Eiffel Tower, *The Smokers* contains lateral curtains and depicts objects from multiple points of view. The volumes of smoke contrast with the flat, angular planes of trees, buildings, and faces. Together these elements function on the picture plane to achieve a decidedly upward movement. Set apart from the dark tonality of urban landscape and foreground figures, the white smoke partakes of an almost sculptural form.

The Smokers is closely related to and slightly earlier in date than *The Wedding*, 1912 (Collection Musée National d'Art Moderne, Paris), and *The Woman in Blue*, late 1912 (Collection Kunstmuseum Basel). Léger's choice of smoke as a subject can be seen within the wider context of an interest on the part of artists at that time in atmospheric phenomena and a wish to give substance to clouds, steam, rain, and snow.

Blaise Cendrars on films and designed sets and costumes for Rolf de Maré's *Ballet Suédois*; in 1923–24 he made his first film without a plot, *Ballet mécanique*. Léger opened an atelier with Amédée Ozenfant in 1924 and in 1925, at the Exposition Internationale des Arts Décoratifs, presented his first murals at Le Corbusier's Pavillon de l'Esprit Nouveau. In 1931 he visited the United States for the first time; in 1935 The Museum of Modern Art, New York, and The Art Institute of Chicago presented exhibitions of his work. Léger lived in the United States from 1940 to 1945 but returned to France after the war. In the decade before his death Léger's wide-ranging projects included book illustrations, monumental figure paintings and murals, stained-glass windows, mosaics, polychrome ceramic sculptures, and set and costume designs. In 1955 he won the Grand Prize at the São Paulo Bienal. Léger died on August 17, 1955, at his home at Gif-sur-Yvette, France. The Musée National Fernand Léger was founded in 1957 in Biot.

23. WOMAN HOLDING A VASE. 1927
(Femme tenant un vase)
Oil on canvas, 57⅝ × 38⅜ in. (146.3 × 97.5 cm.)
Acquired 1958

Woman Holding a Vase is an outstanding example of Léger's attempt to treat human figures with the same plasticity as objects or machines. The arms, the hands, the hair, the breast are all translated into inanimate "values of plastic form." The woman is no longer a figure but an architecture of forms. The interpenetration of woman and vase within an undefined space produces a monumental image.

There are two other very similar versions of *Woman Holding a Vase*: one, dated 1924, is in the Statens Museum for Kunst, Copenhagen; the other, dated 1924–27, is in the Kunstmuseum Basel. Léger indicated that the Guggenheim's painting is the final version.

24. THE GREAT PARADE. 1954
(La Grande parade, état définitif)
Oil on canvas, 117¾ × 157½ in. (299 × 400 cm.)
Acquired 1962

This final version of *The Great Parade*, painted a year before the artist's death, is considered the definitive work of Léger's career. It is the culmination of several themes developed over the preceding fifteen years in paintings such as *Cyclists, Constructors, Country Outings,* and, above all, the *Circus* pictures.

Starting in 1947 Léger made hundreds of preparatory studies for the figures in *The Great Parade*, carefully working out every detail. Earlier painted versions of the subject are in the collections of the Galerie Louise Leiris in Paris (1952) and the Musée National Fernand Léger in Biot (*The Great Parade Against a Red Background*, 1953). In the Guggenheim's *Great Parade* the acrobats at the upper left can be traced back to a 1940 drawing, and the letter "c" in the middle of the canvas is all that remains from earlier versions in which the word *"cirque"* is spelled out. Léger has imposed free color areas that function independently of the essentially linear figurative composition. He has evolved a synthesis of color, form, and rhythm. Not only the immense scale of the final version of *The Great Parade* but the complexity and monumentality of its composition demonstrate Léger's sophistication and command of expression.

COLORPLATES

Pissarro • Manet • Degas • Renoir • Seurat • Cézanne • Van Gogh • Gauguin • Toulouse-Lautrec • Rousseau •
Vuillard • Bonnard • Maillol • Munch • Matisse • Braque • Picasso • Léger

1. CAMILLE PISSARRO *The Hermitage at Pontoise.* c. 1867

2. EDOUARD MANET *Before the Mirror.* 1876

5. GEORGES SEURAT *Seated Woman*. 1883

6. PAUL CÉZANNE *Man with Crossed Arms:* c. 1899

8. PAUL GAUGUIN *In the Vanilla Grove, Man and Horse.* 1891

13. ARISTIDE MAILLOL *Pomona with Lowered Arms.* Late 1920s

14. EDVARD MUNCH *Sketch of the Model Posing.* 1893

16. GEORGES BRAQUE *Landscape near Antwerp. 1906*

19. PABLO PICASSO *Woman Ironing*. 1904

22. FERNAND LÉGER *The Smokers.* 1911–12

COMMENTARIES

Gleizes • Gris • Picabia • Duchamp • Kupka • Delaunay • Kirchner • Nolde • Kokoschka • Schiele • Jawlensky • Kandinsky • Marc • Klee • Feininger • Severini • Chagall • Brancusi • Modigliani

ALBERT GLEIZES

1881–1953. Albert Gleizes was born in Paris on December 8, 1881. While serving in the army from 1901 to 1905, Gleizes began to paint seriously. He exhibited for the first time at the Salon de la Société Nationale des Beaux-Arts, Paris, in 1902, and participated in the Salon d'Automne in 1903 and 1904. With several friends, including the writer René Arcos, Gleizes founded the Abbaye de Créteil outside Paris in 1906. This utopian community of artists and writers scorned bourgeois society and sought to create a nonallegorical, epic art based on modern themes. The Abbaye closed due to financial difficulties in 1908. In 1909 and 1910 Gleizes met Henri Le Fauconnier, Léger, Robert Delaunay, and Jean Metzinger. In 1910 he exhibited at the Salon des Indépendants, Paris, and with the newly formed Jack of Diamonds group in Moscow; the following year he wrote the first of many articles. In collaboration with Metzinger, Gleizes wrote *Du Cubisme*, published in 1912. That same year he helped found the Section d'Or salon.

In 1914 Gleizes again saw military service. His paintings had become abstract by 1915. Travels to New York, Barcelona, and Bermuda during the next four years influenced his stylistic evolution. His first one-man show was held at the Galeries Dalmau, Barcelona, in 1916. Beginning in 1918 Gleizes became deeply involved in a search for spiritual values; his religious concerns were reflected in his painting and writing. In 1927 he founded Moly-Sabata, another utopian community of artists and craftsmen, in Sablons. His book *La Forme et l'histoire* examines Romanesque, Celtic, and Oriental art. In the thirties Gleizes participated in the Abstraction-Création group, an artists' alliance in Paris whose adherents embraced a variety of abstract styles. Later in his career he executed several large commissions including the murals for the Paris Exposition des Arts of 1937. In 1947 a major Gleizes retrospective took place in Lyon at the Chapelle du Lycée Ampère. From 1949 to 1950 Gleizes worked on illustrations for Blaise Pascal's *Pensées*. Gleizes died in Avignon on June 23, 1953.

25. BROOKLYN BRIDGE. 1915
Oil and gouache on canvas, 40⅛ × 40⅛ in.
(102 × 102 cm.)
Acquired 1944

Gleizes arrived in New York for the first time in the autumn of 1915 and stayed there until late in the spring of 1916. He was fascinated with the New York skyline and the signs and colored lights of Broadway. He particularly admired the Brooklyn Bridge and compared its builder to the architect of Notre Dame in Paris. The suspension bridge linking lower Manhattan and Brooklyn was completed in 1883 and inspired numerous other artists—most notably Lyonel Feininger, Joseph Stella, John Marin, and Max Weber—to represent its cables and arches. In the Guggenheim's painting Gleizes evokes this remarkable engineering achievement by means of intersecting diagonals and expresses his own excitement through the boldness and immediacy of his dynamic composition.

In addition to this canvas Gleizes painted two other versions of the Brooklyn Bridge: the final one, produced during a later visit in 1917, is also in the Guggenheim Museum collection.

JUAN GRIS 1887–1927. Juan Gris was born José Victoriano Carmelo Carlos González-Pérez in Madrid on March 23, 1887. He studied mechanical drawing at the Escuela de Artes y Manufacturas in Madrid from 1902 to 1904, during which time he contributed drawings to local periodicals. From 1904 to 1905 he studied painting with the academic artist José Maria Carbonero. In 1906 he moved to Paris, where he lived for most of the remainder of his life. His friends in Paris included Picasso, Braque, Léger, and the writers Max Jacob, Apollinaire, and Maurice Raynal. Although he continued to submit humorous illustrations to journals such as *L'Assiette au beurre, Le Charivari*, and *Le Cri de Paris*, Gris began to paint seriously in 1910. By 1912 he had developed a personal Cubist style.

He exhibited for the first time in 1912: at the Salon des Indépendants in Paris, the Galeries Dalmau in Barcelona, the gallery of Der Sturm in Berlin, the Salon de la Société Normande de Peinture Moderne in Rouen, and the Salon de la Section d'Or in Paris. That same year D.-H. Kahnweiler signed Gris to a contract which gave him exclusive rights to the artist's work. Gris became a good friend of Matisse in 1914 and over the next several years formed close relationships with Jacques Lipchitz and Metzinger. After Kahnweiler fled Paris at the outbreak of World War I, Gris signed a contract with Léonce Rosenberg in 1916. His first major one-man show was held at Rosenberg's Galerie l'Effort Moderne in Paris in 1919. The following year Kahnweiler returned and once again became Gris's dealer.

In 1922 the painter began commissions for sets and costumes for Sergei Diaghilev's Ballets Russes. Gris articulated most of his aesthetic theories during 1924 and 1925. He delivered his definitive lecture, "Des possibilités de la peinture," at the Sorbonne in 1924. Major Gris exhibitions took place at the Galerie Simon in Paris and the Galerie Flechtheim in Berlin in 1923, and at the Galerie Flechtheim in Düsseldorf in 1925. As his health declined, Gris made frequent visits to the Midi in the south of France. He died in Boulogne-sur-Seine on May 11, 1927, at the age of forty.

26. HOUSES IN PARIS. 1911
(Maisons à Paris)
Oil on canvas, 20⅝ × 13½ in. (52.4 × 34.2 cm.)
Acquired 1948

This urban landscape dates from 1911, when Gris lived in Montmartre in Paris. Soon after his arrival there from Madrid in 1906 he settled at 13, rue Ravignan, in the building called the "Bateau-Lavoir," where his compatriot Picasso also lived. Although Braque and Picasso were his friends, Gris was by no means their follower. His stylistic development evolved toward Cubism in an individual manner and revealed the influence of Cézanne. He painted his first oils in 1911. At that time Gris had his studio on the first floor of the "Bateau-Lavoir," overlooking place Ravignan (now place Emile Goudeau), and *Houses in Paris* may well represent the surrounding area.

The Guggenheim's picture reflects this early moment in Gris's Cubism in the slight flattening of the building, the tilted angle at which architectural elements are presented, in the emphasis on line as an integral part of the design, and in the gray tonality which incorporates subtle shades of blue, green, and pink.

Related works showing buildings in Paris include an oil, *Houses in Paris*, in the Sprengel Collection, Hannover, and a drawing in The Museum of Modern Art, New York, Joan and Lester Avnet Collection.

FRANCIS PICABIA

1879–1953. François-Marie-Martinez Picabia was born on or about January 22, 1879, in Paris, of a Spanish father and French mother. He was enrolled at the Ecole des Arts Décoratifs in Paris from 1895 to 1897 and later studied with Albert Charles Wallet, Ferdinand Humbert, and Fernand Cormon. He began to paint in an Impressionist manner in the winter of 1902–3 and started to exhibit works in this style at the Salon d'Automne and the Salon des Indépendants of 1903. His first one-man show was held at the Galerie Haussmann, Paris, in 1905. Starting in 1908, elements of Fauvism, Neo-Impressionism, Cubism, and other forms of abstraction appeared in his painting, and by 1912 he had evolved a personal amalgam of Cubism and Fauvism. He produced his first purely abstract work in 1912.

Picabia became friends with Marcel Duchamp and Apollinaire and associated with members of the Puteaux group in 1911–12. He participated in the 1913 Armory Show, visiting New York on this occasion and frequenting avant-garde circles. Alfred Stieglitz gave him a one-man exhibition at his gallery "291" that same year. In 1915, which marked the beginning of Picabia's machinist or mechanomorphic period, he and Duchamp, among others, instigated and participated in Dada manifestations in New York. Picabia lived in Barcelona in 1916–17; in 1917 he published his first volume of poetry and the first issues of *391*, a magazine he modeled after Stieglitz's periodical *291*. For the next few years Picabia remained involved with the Dadaists in Zürich and Paris, creating scandals at the Salon d'Automne, but finally denounced Dada in 1921 for no longer being "new." He moved to Tremblay-sur-Mauldre, outside of Paris, the following year and returned to figurative art. In 1924 he attacked the poet and critic André Breton and the Surrealists in *391*.

Picabia moved again in 1925, this time to Mougins. During the thirties he became close friends with Gertrude Stein. By the end of World War II Picabia returned to Paris. He resumed painting in an abstract style and writing poetry, and in March 1949 a retrospective of his work was held at the Galerie René Drouin in Paris. Picabia died in Paris on November 30, 1953.

27. THE CHILD CARBURETOR. 1919

(L'Enfant carburateur)
Oil, enamel, metallic paint, gold leaf, pencil, and crayon on stained plywood, 49¾ × 39⅞ in. (126.3 × 101.3 cm.)
Acquired 1955

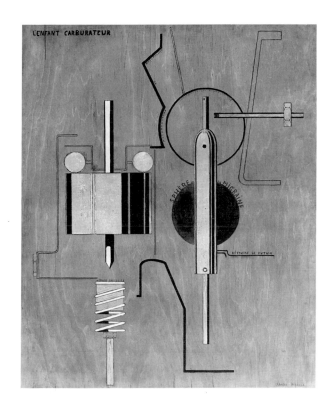

Picabia's machinist style, which emerged in the summer of 1915 in New York and lasted until 1922, reflects his search for machine equivalents or symbols to comment on man. Picabia's love of cars is well known, as is his adaptation of technical diagrams of machines in his paintings. *The Child Carburetor* is based upon the diagram of an actual carburetor, specifically the Racing Claudel. The carburetor's parts can readily be interpreted in sexual terms. Picabia has altered the actual diagram to suggest two sets of male and female sex organs and to produce a machine that could not work. Not only the forms but also the inscriptions reinforce symbolic meaning and sexual imagery. Nor is the artist's personal life irrelevant, for in the autumn of 1919 both Picabia's wife and his mistress gave birth to his children.

Marcel Duchamp

1887–1968. Henri-Robert-Marcel Duchamp was born on July 28, 1887, near Blainville, France. He joined his artist brothers, Jacques Villon and Raymond Duchamp-Villon, in Paris in 1904, where he studied painting at the Académie Julian until 1905. Duchamp's early works were Post-Impressionist in style, and he exhibited for the first time in 1909 at the Salon des Indépendants and the Salon d'Automne in Paris. His paintings of 1911 were directly related to Cubism but emphasized successive images of a single body in motion. In 1912 he painted the first version of *Nude Descending a Staircase*; this was shown at the Salon de la Section d'Or that same year and subsequently created great controversy at the Armory Show in New York in 1913. The Futurist show at Galerie Bernheim-Jeune, Paris, in 1912 impressed him profoundly.

Duchamp's radical and iconoclastic ideas predated the founding of the Dada movement in Zürich in 1915. By 1913 he had abandoned traditional painting and drawing for various experimental forms including mechanical drawings, studies, and notations that would be incorporated in his major work, *The Large Glass (The Bride Stripped Bare by Her Bachelors, Even)* of 1915–23. In 1914 Duchamp introduced his "readymades"—common objects, sometimes altered, presented as works of art—which had a revolutionary impact upon many painters and sculptors. In 1915 Duchamp went to New York, where his circle included Man Ray and Katherine Dreier, with whom he founded the Société Anonyme, as well as Louise and Walter Arensberg, Picabia, and other avant-garde figures.

After playing chess avidly for nine months in Buenos Aires, Duchamp returned to France in the summer of 1919 and associated with the Dada group in Paris. In New York in 1920 he made his first motor-driven constructions and invented Rrose Sélavy, his feminine alter ego. Duchamp moved back to Paris in 1923 and seemed to have abandoned art for chess but in fact continued his artistic experiments. Starting in the mid-1930s he collaborated with the Surrealists and participated in their exhibitions. Duchamp settled permanently in New York in 1942 and became a United States citizen in 1955. During the 1940s he associated and exhibited with the Surrealist emigrés in New York and in 1946 began *Etant donnés*, a major assemblage on which he worked secretly for the next twenty years. Duchamp directly influenced a generation of young Americans. He died in the Paris suburb of Neuilly-sur-Seine on October 2, 1968.

28. Apropos of Little Sister. October 1911
(A propos de jeune soeur)
Oil on canvas, 28¾ × 23⅝ in. (73 × 60 cm.)
Acquired 1971

The sitter is Magdeleine, the youngest of Marcel Duchamp's brothers and sisters, who was thirteen at the time this portrait was done. She remembers that she was reading while Duchamp painted her. During the autumn of 1911 Duchamp portrayed his sister in profile in another picture, *Yvonne and Magdeleine Torn in Tatters*, and completed *Sonata*, which represents his mother and three sisters. In *Apropos of Little Sister* the delicate, light colors are accentuated by the texture of the canvas itself, and the angularity of forms suggests an awareness of Cubism. Painted at his family home in Rouen in October 1911, it follows Duchamp's early work, which was influenced by Cézanne, the Fauves, and the Symbolists, but occurs before his interest in successive images of a single body in motion culminated early in 1912 in *Nude Descending a Staircase*.

František Kupka 1871–1957.

František Kupka was born on September 22, 1871, in Opočno in eastern Bohemia. From 1889 to 1892 he studied at the Prague Academy. During that time he painted historical and patriotic themes. In 1892 Kupka enrolled at the Akademie der bildenden Künste in Vienna, where he concentrated on symbolic and allegorical subjects. He exhibited at the Kunstverein, Vienna, in 1894. His involvement with Theosophy and Eastern philosophy dates from this period. By the spring of 1896 Kupka had settled in Paris, where he attended the Académie Julian briefly before studying with J. P. Laurens at the Ecole des Beaux-Arts.

Kupka worked as an illustrator of books and posters and, during his early years in Paris, became known for his satirical drawings appearing in newspapers and magazines. In 1906 he settled in Puteaux, a suburb of Paris, and that same year exhibited for the first time at the Salon d'Automne. Kupka was deeply impressed by the first Futurist Manifesto, published in 1909 in *Le Figaro*. His work became increasingly abstract about 1910–11, reflecting his theories of motion, color, and the relationship between music and painting. In 1911 he participated in meetings of the Puteaux group, which included his neighbors Jacques Villon and Raymond Duchamp-Villon as well as Duchamp, Gleizes, Metzinger, Picabia, Léger, Apollinaire, and others. In 1912 he exhibited at the Salon des Indépendants in the Cubist room, although he did not wish to be identified with any movement. Later that year at the Salon d'Automne his paintings caused critical indignation.

La Création dans les arts plastiques (Creation in the Visual Arts), a book Kupka completed in 1913, was published in Prague in 1923. In 1921 his first one-man show in Paris was held at Galerie Povolozky. In 1931 he was a founding member of the Abstraction-Création group together with Theo van Doesburg, Auguste Herbin, Georges Vantongerloo, Jean Hélion, Jean Arp, and Gleizes; in 1936 his work was included in the exhibition "Cubism and Abstract Art" at The Museum of Modern Art, New York, and in an important two-man show with Alphonse Mucha at the Jeu de Paume, Paris. A major retrospective of his work took place at the Galerie S.V.U. Mánes in Prague in 1946. That same year Kupka participated in the Salon des Réalités Nouvelles, Paris, where he continued to exhibit regularly until his death. During the early 1950s he gained general recognition and had several one-man shows in New York. He died in Puteaux on June 24, 1957. Important Kupka retrospectives were held at the Musée National d'Art Moderne, Paris, in 1958 and The Solomon R. Guggenheim Museum, New York, in 1975.

29. PLANES BY COLORS, LARGE NUDE
1909–10
(Plans par couleurs, grand nu)
Oil on canvas, 59⅛ × 71⅛ in. (150.1 × 180.8 cm.)
Gift, Mrs. Andrew P. Fuller, 1968

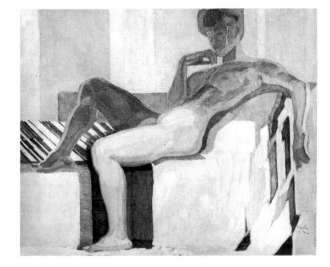

Over a period of several years, from about 1906 to 1910, Kupka transformed the traditional reclining nude into a formal arrangement of color planes: *Planes by Colors, Large Nude* represents one stage in this metamorphosis. The evolution of this painting can be traced through more than twenty studies.

Although his work reveals a familiarity with Divisionism, Symbolism, Fauvism, and Cubism, Kupka was not allied with any artistic movement. In *Planes by Colors, Large Nude* Kupka has eliminated three-dimensional modeling and has constructed the figure with color areas. The pinkish white, green, and purple planes differentiate successive positions in depth, al-though spatial recession is not otherwise indicated. It is a pivotal work, which points in the direction of abstraction and would be followed by other paintings in which Kupka investigated planes of color.

ROBERT DELAUNAY 1885–1941. Robert-Victor-Félix Delaunay was born in Paris on April 12, 1885. In 1902, after completing his secondary education, he apprenticed in a studio for theater sets in Belleville. In 1903 he started painting and by 1904 was exhibiting: that year and in 1906 at the Salon d'Automne and from 1904 until World War I at the Salon des Indépendants. Between 1905 and 1907 Delaunay became friendly with Rousseau and Metzinger and studied the color theories of M.-E. Chevreul; he was then painting in a Neo-Impressionist manner. Cézanne's work also influenced Delaunay about this time. From 1907–8 he served in the military in Laon and upon returning to Paris he had contact with the Cubists, who in turn influenced his work. The years 1909–10 saw the emergence of Delaunay's personal style: he painted his first Eiffel Tower—a recurrent theme in his work—in 1909. In 1910 he married the painter Sonia Terk, who became his collaborator on many projects.

Delaunay's participation in exhibitions in Germany and his association with advanced artists working there began in 1911: that year Vasily Kandinsky invited him to participate in the first Blaue Reiter (Blue Rider) exhibition in Munich. At this time he became friendly with Apollinaire, Henri Le Fauconnier, and Gleizes. In 1912 Delaunay's

30. SAINT-SÉVERIN NO. 3. 1909–10
Oil on canvas, 45 × 34⅞ in. (114.1 × 88.6 cm.)
Gift, Solomon R. Guggenheim, 1941

Delaunay executed seven large oils and numerous drawings of the church of Saint-Séverin in 1909–10: the first instance of a series in his work. The Gothic church, located in rue des Prêtres Saint-Séverin in Paris, interested the young artist, who painted the canvases in his nearby studio. Like the other versions, Saint-Séverin No. 3 represents the fifteenth-century ambulatory with its curved vaults, Gothic arches, and stained-glass windows. Delaunay chose a view—at the point where the ambulatory curves around the choir—that enabled him to depict tipping arches and bulging columns and at the same time to paint colors modified by the light emanating from the stained-glass windows. The monochromatic color of the Guggenheim's picture is reminiscent of Cézanne's palette. In fact, Delaunay spoke of the Saint-Séverin motif as occurring in "a period of transition from Cézanne to Cubism, or rather from Cézanne to the Windows." (R. Delaunay, Du Cubisme à l'art abstrait, ed. P. Francastel, Paris, 1957, pp. 86–87.)

first one-man show took place at the Galerie Barbazanges, Paris, and he began his Window pictures. Inspired by the lyricism of color in these paintings, Apollinaire invented the term "Orphism," or "Orphic Cubism," to describe Delaunay's work. In 1913 Delaunay painted his Circular Form, or Disc, pictures; this year also marked the beginning of his friendship with Blaise Cendrars.

From 1914 to 1920 Delaunay lived in Spain and Portugal and became friends with Sergei Diaghilev, Igor Stravinsky, Diego Rivera, and Léonide Massine. He did the decor for the Ballets Russes in 1918. By 1920 he had returned to Paris. There, in 1922, a major exhibition of his work was held at Galerie Paul Guillaume, and he began his second Eiffel Tower series. In 1924 he undertook his Runner paintings and in 1925 executed frescoes for the Palais de l'Ambassade de France at the Exposition Internationale des Arts Décoratifs in Paris. In 1937 he completed murals for the Palais des Chemins de Fer and Palais de l'Air at the Paris World's Fair. His last works were decorations for the sculpture hall of the Salon des Tuileries in 1938. In 1939 he helped organize the exhibition "Réalités Nouvelles." Delaunay died in Montpellier on October 25, 1941.

31. SIMULTANEOUS WINDOWS (2ND MOTIF, 1ST PART). 1912
(Les Fenêtres simultanées [2ᵉ motif, 1ʳᵉ partie])
Oil on canvas, 21⅝ × 18¼ in. (55.2 × 46.3 cm.)
Gift, Solomon R. Guggenheim, 1941

Simultaneous Windows (2nd Motif, 1st Part) is one of a series of at least seventeen oils Delaunay painted in 1912. By means of overlapping transparent planes of pure color, he has built up the triangular organization of *Windows*. Although these planes are set down in an orderly sequence, their contrasting shades of blue, green, and purple are meant to be perceived simultaneously.

Delaunay was aware of Chevreul's theories involving complementary colors and simultaneous contrasts in color harmony. Moreover, simultaneity was a popular concept about 1912 to 1914, and the term was used not only by painters but by writers and musicians as well. Delaunay wrote: "I have dared to create an architecture of color, and have hoped to realize the impulses, the state of a dynamic poetry while remaining completely within the painterly medium, free from all literature, from all descriptive anecdote. . . . Color, the fruit of light, is the foundation of the painter's means of painting—and its language." (G. Vriesen and M. Imdahl, *Robert Delaunay: Light and Color*, New York, 1969, p. 42.) Delaunay's *Windows* inspired the poet Apollinaire to write *Les Fenêtres*.

ERNST LUDWIG KIRCHNER

1880–1938. Ernst Ludwig Kirchner was born on May 6, 1880, in Aschaffenburg, Germany. After years of travel his family settled in Chemnitz in 1890. From 1901 to 1905 he studied architecture at the Dresden Technische Hochschule and pictorial art in Munich at the Kunsthochschule and an experimental art school established by Wilhelm von Debschitz and Hermann Obrist. While in Munich he produced his first woodcuts; the graphic arts were to become as important to him as painting. At this time he was drawn to Neo-Impressionism as well as to the old masters.

In 1905 Kirchner together with Fritz Bleyl, Karl Schmidt-Rottluff, and Erich Heckel formed an association in Dresden known as Die Brücke (Bridge), whose members shared an interest in the graphic arts and an admiration for the work of Munch and Van Gogh. The group was later joined by Cuno Amiet, Max Pechstein, Emil Nolde, and Otto Müller. From 1905 to 1910 Dresden hosted exhibitions of Post-Impressionists, including Van Gogh, as well as shows of Munch, Gustav Klimt, and the Fauves, which deeply impressed Kirchner. Other important influences were Japanese prints, the Ajanta wall paintings, and African and Oceanic art. Kirchner moved to Berlin with the Brücke group in 1911. The following year Franz Marc invited the Brücke artists to participate in the second show of the Blaue Reiter (Blue Rider) in Munich. In 1913 Kirchner exhibited in the Armory Show in New York, in Chicago and Boston, and was given his first one-man shows in Germany, at the Folkwang Museum of Hagen and the Galerie Gurlitt in Berlin. That same year also marked the dissolution of the Brücke.

During World War I Kirchner was discharged from the army because of a nervous and physical collapse. He was treated at Dr. Kohnstamm's sanatorium in Königstein near Frankfurt, where he completed five wall frescoes in 1916. The artist was severely injured when struck by an automobile in 1917; the next year, during his long period of recuperation, he settled in Frauenkirch near Davos, Switzerland, where he hoped to form a progressive artistic community. Although his plans did not materialize, many young artists, particularly those of the Basel-based Rot-Blau (Red-Blue) group, sought him out during the twenties for guidance. One-man shows of Kirchner's work were held throughout the thirties in Munich, Bern, Hamburg, Basel, Detroit, and New York. However, physical deterioration and mental anxiety overtook him again in the middle of the decade. His inclusion in the 1937 Nazi-sponsored show of *Entartete Kunst* (degenerate art) in Munich caused him further distress. Kirchner died by his own hand on June 15, 1938.

32. GERDA, HALF-LENGTH PORTRAIT. 1914
(Frauenkopf, Gerda)
Oil on canvas, 39 × 29⅝ in. (99.1 × 75.3 cm.)
Partial Gift, Mr. and Mrs. Mortimer M. Denker, 1978

Kirchner painted *Gerda, Half-Length Portrait* in Berlin before the outbreak of World War I. Like her younger sister Erna, who was to become the artist's common-law wife, Gerda Schilling was a dancer. In this picture her assertive pose is enhanced by the angular stylizations in the background, the hatched patterning of the brushstrokes, and the tension between the representation of three-dimensional forms and the two-dimensional picture plane. *Gerda, Half-Length Portrait* shares with Kirchner's Berlin street scenes of 1913–14 not only subject matter but also the intensity and dissonance of color and the use of the background as a dynamic design element.

EMIL NOLDE 1867–1956.

Emil Nolde was born Emil Hansen on August 7, 1867, in North Schleswig, near Nolde, Germany. He worked as an ornamental carver in furniture factories in Munich, Karlsruhe, and Berlin from 1888 to 1890. After a sojourn in Berlin he moved to St. Gallen, Switzerland, in 1891, where he taught ornamental drawing and modeling at the Industrie und Gewerbemuseum. He studied art with Friedrich Fehr in Munich in 1898 and at the Hölzel-Schule in Dachau in 1899, before visiting Paris in the fall of that year to attend the Académie Julian. After stays in Copenhagen, Berlin, and Flensburg, Germany, he settled in 1903 on the island of Alsen.

In 1905, after Nolde returned from a trip to Italy, his first one-man show was held at the Galerie Ernst Arnold in Dresden. From 1906 to 1907 he belonged to the Dresden-based Brücke (Bridge) group of artists. Nolde moved to Dresden in 1907 and developed friendships with Kirchner, Max Pechstein, and Erich Heckel. That same year the Museum Folkwang in Hagen and the Galerie Commeter in Hamburg presented solo exhibitions of his work. The Berlin Secession, which had rejected Nolde's Expressionist paintings for several years, expelled him in 1910 after he criticized the association's president. In 1912 he participated in the Sonderbund exhibition in Cologne and the second show of the Blaue Reiter (Blue Rider) in Munich. From 1913 to 1914 he traveled across Russia and the Far East to New Guinea. He settled in Berlin in 1915 and spent most winters there until 1940. In 1927 an important traveling retrospective was organized in Dresden, followed the next year by a major one-man show at the Kunsthalle Basel. Nolde's paintings were confiscated by the Nazis in 1937 and he was forbidden to paint, despite his support of the regime. Nolde's first one-man show in the United States was held at Curt Valentin's Buchholz Gallery in New York in 1939. The Kestner-Gesellschaft of Hannover presented a retrospective of his work in 1948. Nolde died on April 13, 1956, in Seebüll, where the Stiftung Seebüll Ada und Emil Nolde was formed shortly thereafter.

33. YOUNG HORSES. 1916
(Junge Pferde)
Oil on canvas, 28½ × 39½ in. (72.4 × 100.3 cm.)
Acquired 1979

In the summer of 1916, during his stay at Utenwarf, Nolde made sketches which he then worked up into oils upon his return to Alsen. There are five canvases representing pairs of horses that date from 1916. The Guggenheim's picture is more abstract than a closely related sketch and another canvas, *Landscape with Young Horses*, both in the Stiftung Seebüll Ada und Emil Nolde.

In this painting two silhouetted shapes of rearing horses stand out against a brooding sky. The green meadow and orange glow at the horizon intensify the dramatic mood. Nolde's landscape resembles the flat, open, rather desolate countryside of his native Schleswig-Holstein. The strong patterns of light and the dark, windswept, overhanging clouds do not merely fill the sky: they impart a mysterious, vital energy and Expressionist force.

OSKAR KOKOSCHKA

OSKAR KOKOSCHKA 1886–1980. Oskar Kokoschka was born on March 1, 1886, in the Austrian town of Pöchlarn. He spent most of his youth in Vienna, where he entered the Kunstgewerbeschule in 1904 or 1905. While still a student he painted fans and postcards for the Wiener Werkstätte (Vienna Workshops), which published his first book of poetry in 1908. That same year Kokoschka was fiercely criticized for the works he exhibited in the Vienna Kunstschau and consequently was dismissed from the Kunstgewerbeschule. At this time he attracted the attention of the architect Adolf Loos, who became his most vigorous supporter. In this early period Kokoschka wrote plays that are considered among the first examples of Expressionist drama.

His first one-man show was held at Paul Cassirer's gallery in Berlin in 1910, followed later that year by another at the Museum Folkwang in Essen. In 1910 he also began to contribute to Herwarth Walden's periodical *Der Sturm*. Kokoschka concentrated on portraiture, dividing his time between Berlin and Vienna from 1910 to 1914. In 1915, shortly after the outbreak of World War I, he volunteered to serve on the eastern front, where he was seriously wounded. Still recuperating in 1917, he settled in Dresden and in 1919 accepted a professorship at the Akademie there. In 1918 Paul Westheim's comprehensive monograph on the artist was published.

Kokoschka traveled extensively during the 1920s and 1930s in Europe, North Africa, and the Middle East. In 1931 he returned to Vienna but, as a result of the Nazis' growing power, he moved to Prague in 1935. He acquired Czechoslovak citizenship two years later. Kokoschka painted a portrait of Czechoslovakia's president Thomas Garrigue Masaryk in 1936, and the two became friends. In 1937 the Nazis condemned his work as "degenerate art" and removed it from public view. The artist fled to England in 1938, the year of his first one-man show in the United States at the Buchholz Gallery in New York. In 1947 he became a British national. Two important traveling shows of Kokoschka's work originated in Boston and Munich in 1948 and 1950 respectively. In 1953 he settled in Villeneuve, near Geneva, and began teaching at the Internationale Sommer Akademie für bildende Kunst, where he initiated his Schule des Sehens, a school of visual arts. Kokoschka's collected writings were published in 1956, and about this time he became involved in stage design. In 1962 he was honored with a retrospective at the Tate Gallery in London. Kokoschka died on February 22, 1980, in Montreux, Switzerland.

34. KNIGHT ERRANT. 1915
(Der irrende Ritter)
Oil on canvas, 35¼ × 70⅛ in. (89.5 × 180.1 cm.)
Acquired 1948

The knight in armor appears strangely suspended above the landscape. Kokoschka has confirmed that the knight is a self-portrait and that the canvas was painted before he served in World War I. While the figure of the knight may dominate the picture, its meaning is amplified by the presence of two small figures within the landscape: in the upper center of the composition a bird-man, who also resembles the artist, is perched on a limb which hangs over the ocean; reclining in the landscape at the right is the sphinx-woman, who represents Kokoschka's mistress, Alma Mahler. Although Kokoschka had previously depicted the bird-man and sphinx-woman close together, here they are separated as if to sym-bolize the end of the artist's relationship with Alma. The cloud-filled sky contains the letters *"ES,"* which undoubtedly refer to Christ's lament: *"Eloi, Eloi, lama sabachthani"* ("My God, my God, why hast Thou forsaken me?"). The agitated brushwork and disturbing colors intensify the tumultuous seascape and emphasize the emotional content of Kokoschka's picture.

EGON SCHIELE

1890–1918. Egon Schiele was born on June 12, 1890, in Tulln, Austria. After attending school in Krems and Klosterneuburg, he enrolled in the Akademie der bildenden Künste in Vienna in 1906. Here he studied painting and drawing but was frustrated by the school's conservatism. In 1907 he met Klimt, who encouraged him and influenced his work. Schiele left the Akademie in 1909 and founded the Neukunstgruppe (New Art Group) with other dissatisfied students. Upon Klimt's invitation Schiele exhibited at the Internationale Kunstschau of 1909 in Vienna, where he encountered the work of Van Gogh, Munch, Jan Toroop, and others. On the occasion of the first exhibition of the Neukunstgruppe in 1909 at the Piska Salon, Vienna, Schiele met the art critic and writer Arthur Roessler, who befriended him and wrote admiringly of his work. In 1910 he began a long friendship with the collector Heinrich Benesch. By this time Schiele had developed a personal Expressionist portrait and landscape style and was receiving a number of portrait commissions from the Viennese intelligentsia.

Seeking isolation, Schiele left Vienna in 1911 to live in a succession of small villages: he concentrated increasingly on self-portraits and allegories of life, death, and sex and produced erotic watercolors. In 1912 he was arrested for "immorality" and "seduction"; during his twenty-four-day imprisonment he executed a number of poignant watercolors and drawings. Schiele participated in various group exhibitions, including those of the Neukunstgruppe in Prague, 1910, and Budapest, 1912; the Sonderbund, Cologne, 1912; and several Secession shows in Munich, beginning in 1911. In 1913 the Galerie Hans Goltz, Munich, mounted Schiele's first one-man show. A one-man exhibition of his work took place in Paris in 1914. The following year Schiele married Edith Harms and was drafted into the Austrian army. He painted prolifically and continued to exhibit during his military service. His one-man show at the Vienna Secession of 1918 brought him critical acclaim and financial success. He died several months later in Vienna, at the age of twenty-eight, on October 31, 1918, a victim of influenza, which had claimed his wife three days earlier.

35. *PORTRAIT OF JOHANN HARMS*. 1916
Oil with wax on canvas, 54½ × 42½ in.
(138.3 × 108 cm.)
Partial Gift, Dr. and Mrs. Otto Kallir, 1969

Johann Harms (1843–1917) became Schiele's father-in-law in June 1915. Schiele's letters record that in April 1916 he made drawings and worked on the canvas for the seventy-three-year-old man's portrait. As is typical of his portraits, there are no props used as clues to the sitter's personality or occupation (in this case that of a master locksmith). While even the chair is sometimes omitted, the one on which Harms sits in this picture was made by Schiele for his studio.

Unlike many Expressionist paintings, the color is somber, almost monochromatic. The color values are used in a hierarchical manner: they build from the dark background to the median gray of the body's bulky diagonal shape and reach their height in the more vibrant head and hands, always the focal points of Schiele's figure paintings. These small areas succinctly embody his exploration of the sitter's character. In this case the rough, skeletal hands and deeply furrowed brow express the weariness of old age. But the pose of the figure, which seems to be draped over the chair because of the low viewpoint, and the tenderness with which the head rests on the hand, soften the image and suggest a melancholy peace.

ALEXEJ JAWLENSKY

1864–1941. Alexej Georgievich Jawlensky was born in or near Torzhok, Russia, on March 13, 1864, and educated in Moscow. He first studied art, while an army lieutenant, at the Academy in St. Petersburg in 1889. In 1896 Jawlensky resigned his military commission to devote himself to painting and moved with Marianne von Werefkin and Helene Nesnakomoff to Munich. From 1896 to 1899 he attended the Ažbe school in Munich, where he first met Kandinsky, who had also recently left Russia.

Jawlensky was included in the Munich and Berlin Secession exhibitions in 1903. About this time he visited Russia, participating in exhibitions there, and traveled in Europe: in 1905 he met Matisse in Paris and his work was included in the Salon d'Automne. In 1907 he met the Nabis Jan Verkade and Sérusier in Munich. Kandinsky and Jawlensky became close friends during the summer of 1908 and the following year the two, together with a number of other artists, founded the Neue Künstlervereinigung München (NKVM, New Artists' Association of Munich). Jawlensky's first one-man exhibition took place in Barmen in 1911. His long friendship with Nolde began in 1912.

The outbreak of World War I forced Jawlensky to flee to Switzerland, where he painted his stylized landscape series, Variations, from 1914 to 1921. In Zürich in 1917 he started his Faces of Saints, or Faces of the Saviour, series and in Ascona in 1918 he began his Constructivist heads. Jawlensky returned to Germany in 1921, settling in Wiesbaden. He married Helene Nesnakomoff, the mother of his twenty-year-old son, in 1922. With Paul Klee, Kandinsky, and Feininger he was part of the Blaue Vier (Blue Four) group, founded in 1924. Jawlensky continued to paint Constructivist heads during the years in Wiesbaden; from 1934 to 1937 he executed his mystical Meditation series. Crippled by arthritis, Jawlensky was finally forced to cease painting by 1938. He died on March 15, 1941, in Wiesbaden.

36. HELENE WITH COLORED TURBAN. 1910
(Helene mit buntem Turban)
Oil on board, 37⅛ × 31⅞ in. (94.2 × 81 cm.)
Acquired 1965

Jawlensky's paintings from 1907 to 1910 combine bold Fauvist color and simplified linear structure with an intense personal feeling for the subject. The monumental *Helene with Colored Turban* is a portrait of Helene Nesnakomoff (c. 1880–1965), who had borne the artist a son in 1902 and whom he was to marry in 1922. This canvas reveals the influence of Matisse's *Red Madras Headdress* (Collection The Barnes Foundation, Merion, Pennsylvania), which is a portrait of Mme Matisse wearing a red turban. Jawlensky has adopted Matisse's brilliant palette and painterly surface treatment but heightens the expressive force of the color and endows the personality of the sitter with an emotional dimension not present in Matisse's work.

On the reverse of this work is *Portrait of a Young Girl* (c. 1909), an oil sketch of Resi, a neighbor of the artist who often posed for him.

Vasily Kandinsky

1866–1944. Vasily Vasilievich Kandinsky was born on December 4, 1866, in Moscow. From 1886 to 1892 he studied law and economics at the University of Moscow, where he lectured after his graduation. In 1896 he declined a teaching position at the University of Dorpat in order to study art in Munich with Anton Ažbe from 1897 to 1899 and at the Akademie with Franz von Stuck in 1900. From 1901 to 1903 Kandinsky taught at the art school of the Phalanx, a group he had cofounded in Munich. One of his students was Gabriele Münter, who remained his companion until 1914. In 1902 Kandinsky exhibited for the first time with the Berlin Secession and produced his first woodcuts. In 1903–4 he began his travels in Italy, the Netherlands, and North Africa as well as his visits to Russia. He showed frequently at the Salon d'Automne in Paris from 1904 onward.

In 1909 Kandinsky was elected president of the newly founded Neue Künstlervereinigung München (NKVM, New Artists' Association of Munich). The group's first show took place at Heinrich Thannhauser's Moderne Galerie in Munich in 1909. In 1911 Kandinsky and Franz Marc withdrew from the NKVM and began to make plans for the Blaue Reiter (Blue Rider) almanac. The first exhibition of the Blaue Reiter was held in December of that year at the Moderne Galerie. Kandinsky published *Über das Geistige in der Kunst (On the Spiritual in Art)* in 1911. In 1912 the second Blaue Reiter show was held at the Galerie Hans Goltz, Munich, and the *Almanach der Blaue Reiter* appeared. Kandinsky's first one-man show was held at the gallery of Der Sturm in Berlin in 1912. In 1913 his works were included in the Armory Show in New York and the Erster Deutscher Herbstsalon (First German Autumn Salon) in Berlin. Except for visits to Scandinavia, Kandinsky lived in Russia from 1914 to 1921, principally in Moscow, where he held a position at the People's Commissariat of Education.

Kandinsky began teaching at the Bauhaus in Weimar in 1922. In 1923 he was given his first one-man show in New York by the Société Anonyme, of which he became vice-president. With Klee, Feininger, and Jawlensky he was part of the Blaue Vier (Blue Four) group, formed in 1924. He moved with the Bauhaus to Dessau in 1925 and became a German citizen in 1928. The Nazi government closed the Bauhaus in 1933 and later that year Kandinsky settled in Neuilly-sur-Seine near Paris; he acquired French citizenship in 1939. Fifty-seven of his works were confiscated by the Nazis in the 1937 purge of *Entartete Kunst* (degenerate art). Kandinsky died on December 13, 1944, in Neuilly.

37. Blue Mountain. 1908–9

(Der blaue Berg)
Oil on canvas, 41¾ × 38 in. (106 × 96.6 cm.)
Gift, Solomon R. Guggenheim, 1941

Kandinsky's earliest work consisted of woodcuts and small impressionistic oil studies done from nature. By 1908 he knew the work of Post-Impressionists such as Gauguin and Van Gogh as well as that of the Nabis, Matisse, and the other Fauves. His paintings demonstrate an affinity with the Jugendstil Arts and Crafts movement and with religious paintings on glass. *Blue Mountain* dates from 1908–9, a transitional period in Kandinsky's career. While identifiable forms can still be discerned in this picture, they have lost their impact as representational images and have moved far in the direction of abstraction. The flattened blue, red, and yellow forms emphasize the upward thrust of the composition.

The motif of three horsemen and a mountain figures prominently in Kandinsky's oeuvre until 1913. As early as 1902 the image of a single horse and rider appeared in his work.

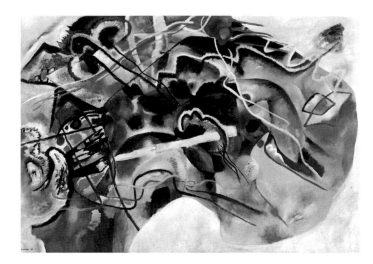

38. PAINTING WITH WHITE BORDER
May 1913
(Das Bild mit weissem Rand)
Oil on canvas, 55¼ × 78⅞ in. (140.3 × 200.3 cm.)
Gift, Solomon R. Guggenheim, 1937

Kandinsky's images became increasingly abstract in the period from 1909 to 1913. He attenuated the forms in his paintings so they ultimately lost their identity as representational images. Consequently, it is difficult to read specific motifs. In his essay on *Painting with White Border*, Kandinsky stated that the picture was a translation of impressions he received on his most recent visit to Moscow. The Russian subject is suggested by the backs of three horses—a troika—at the upper left. The central motif is a knight (identified as St. George) on horseback with a long white lance attacking a serpent or dragon at the lower left. This image, as well as others that Kandinsky used in paintings of the Last Judgment, Resurrection, and All Saints' Day, appears clearly in the numerous studies for the painting but is sublimated into abstract forms in this final version. The white border is Kandinsky's solution to a compositional problem in completing the picture.

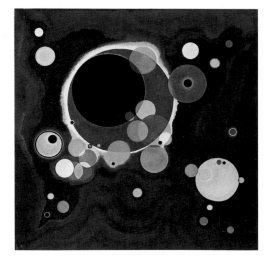

39. SEVERAL CIRCLES. 1926
(Einige Kreise)
Oil on canvas, 55¼ × 55⅜ in. (140.3 × 140.7 cm.)
Gift, Solomon R. Guggenheim, 1941

Circles first occurred in Kandinsky's work in 1921 and soon assumed a major role in his pictures. They are clearly the dominant motif in *Several Circles* of 1926. From the dark gray, amorphous, nebular environment emerges a primary form—the large dark blue circle surrounded by a corona. A black disc is enclosed within the larger blue one and their circumferences meet at a tangent. From this matrix many colored circles are successively generated. They resemble transparent gels. Those circles that overlap with others change color at the point of intersection.

The circle is the most elementary form. Kandinsky wrote that "the circle is the synthesis of the greatest oppositions. It combines the concentric and the excentric in a single form, and in equilibrium." (W. Grohmann, *Wassily Kandinsky: Life and Work,* New York, 1958, p. 188.) For Kandinsky the circle represents a development in cosmic evolution parallel to that of spirit taking the form of matter.

Franz Marc

1880–1916. Franz Marc was born on February 8, 1880, in Munich. The son of a landscape painter, he decided to become an artist after a year of military service interrupted his plans to study philology. From 1900 to 1902 he studied at the Akademie in Munich with Gabriel von Hackl and Wilhelm von Diez. The following year, during a visit to France, he was introduced to Japanese woodcuts and the work of the Impressionists in Paris.

Marc suffered from severe depressions from 1904 to 1907, the year his father died. In 1907 he traveled again to Paris, where he responded enthusiastically to the work of Van Gogh, Gauguin, the Cubists, and the Expressionists; later he was impressed by the Matisse exhibition in Munich in 1910. During this period he received steady income from the animal anatomy lessons he gave to artists.

In 1910 his first one-man show was held at the Kunsthandlung Brackl in Munich, and Marc met August Macke and the collector Bernhard Koehler. He publicly defended the Neue Künstlervereinigung München (NKVM, New Artists' Association of Munich), and was formally welcomed into the group in 1911, when he met Kandinsky. After internal dissension split the NKVM, he and Kandinsky began to make plans for the Blaue Reiter (Blue Rider) almanac; the first Blaue Reiter exhibition took place in December 1911 at Heinrich Thannhauser's Moderne Galerie in Munich. Marc invited members of the Berlin Brücke (Bridge) group to participate in the second Blaue Reiter show two months later at the Galerie Hans Goltz in Munich. The *Almanach der Blaue Reiter* was published with lead articles by Marc in May 1912. When World War I broke out in August 1914, Marc immediately enlisted. He was deeply troubled by Macke's death in action shortly thereafter; during the war he produced his *Sketchbook from the Field*. Marc died at Verdun on March 4, 1916.

40. Yellow Cow. 1911
(Gelbe Kuh)
Oil on canvas, 55⅜ × 74½ in. (140.5 × 189.2 cm.)
Acquired 1949

Yellow Cow, painted in Sindelsdorf, was shown at the first Blaue Reiter exhibition, which opened in Munich on December 18, 1911. It is an early example of Marc's mature style. The sculptured, clearly defined volumes of the cow show a transitional stage between the artist's earlier more naturalistic treatment of his subject matter and his later stylized flattening of objects into planes. Similarly, the full rounded contours and arabesques that dominate the composition would soon be replaced by more concise geometric forms.

The colors have a symbolic value and should be seen in relation to Marc's theories. In his correspondence with August Macke in December 1910, Marc specified that "blue is the *male* principle, severe, bitter, spiritual, and intellectual. Yellow is the *female* principle, gentle, cheerful, and sensual. Red is *matter*, brutal and heavy, the color which must be fought and overcome by the other two!" (A. Z. Rudenstine, *The Guggenheim Museum Collection: Paintings 1880–1945*, New York, 1976, p. 493.) He proceeded to elaborate on various combinations of colors and their meanings.

There is an oil sketch for *Yellow Cow* in a private collection, and an almost identical yellow cow appears in a painting of 1912, *Cows Red, Green, Yellow*, in the Städtische Galerie im Lenbachhaus, Munich.

PAUL KLEE 1879–1940. Paul Klee was born on December 18, 1879, in Münchenbuchsee, Switzerland, into a family of musicians. His childhood love of music was always to remain profoundly important in his life and work. From 1898 to 1901 Klee studied in Munich, first with Heinrich Knirr, then at the Akademie under Franz von Stuck. Upon completing his schooling, he traveled to Italy; this was the first in a series of trips abroad that nourished his visual sensibilities. He settled in Bern in 1902. A series of his satirical etchings was exhibited at the Munich Secession in 1906. That same year Klee married and moved to Munich. There he gained exposure to modern art; he saw the work of James Ensor, Cézanne, Van Gogh, and Matisse. Klee's work was shown at the Kunstmuseum Bern in 1910 and at Heinrich Thannhauser's Moderne Galerie in Munich in 1911. Klee met Kandinsky, August Macke, Marc, Jawlensky, and other avant-garde figures in 1911; he participated in important shows of advanced art, including the second Blaue Reiter (Blue Rider) exhibition, 1912, and the Erster Deutscher Herbstsalon (First German Autumn Salon), 1913. In 1912 he visited Paris for the second time, where he saw the work of Picasso and Braque and met Robert Delaunay. Klee helped found the Neue Münchner Secession in 1914. Color became central to his art only after a revelatory trip to North Africa in 1914.

In 1920 a major Klee retrospective was held at the Galerie Hans Goltz, Munich, his *Schöpferische Konfession (Creative Credo)* was published, and he was appointed to the faculty of the Bauhaus. Klee taught at the Bauhaus in Weimar from 1921 to 1926 and in Dessau from 1926 to 1931. During his tenure he was in close contact with other Bauhaus masters such as Kandinsky, Feininger, and László Moholy-Nagy. In 1924 the Blaue Vier (Blue Four), consisting of Klee, Kandinsky, Feininger, and Jawlensky, was founded. Among his notable exhibitions of this period were his first in the United States at the Société Anonyme, New York, 1924; his first major show in Paris the following year at the Galerie Vavin-Raspail; and an exhibition at The Museum of Modern Art, New York, 1930. Klee went to Düsseldorf to teach at the Akademie in 1931, shortly before the Nazis closed the Bauhaus. Forced by the Nazis to leave his position in Düsseldorf in 1933, Klee settled in Bern. Major Klee exhibitions took place in Bern and Basel in 1935 and in Zürich in 1940. Klee died on June 29, 1940, in Muralto-Locarno, Switzerland.

41. THE BAVARIAN DON GIOVANNI. 1919
(Der bayrische Don Giovanni)
Watercolor on paper, 8⅞ × 8⅜ in. (22.5 × 21.3 cm.)
Acquired 1941

Klee's love of music is well known and is expressed visually throughout his work. Mozart and Bach were his favorite composers and he knew the score of *Don Giovanni*. In the 1920s Klee wanted to design new sets for a production of the opera in Dresden but this project was never undertaken.

Klee painted *The Bavarian Don Giovanni* while he was still living in Munich in Bavaria. The flat, rectilinear organization divides the surface into triangular-shaped colored planes, reminiscent of those in Robert Delaunay's *Windows* (1912), a painting Klee admired. Yet here the planes can be seen as theatrical curtains that force the viewer to shift from the realm of visual perception to that of the imagination. The ladders link one part of the composition to another and also lead to the names written on the paper. These names, though not derived from Mozart's *Don Giovanni*, are characteristically Bavarian, and might refer to girls Klee once knew. Associative and pictorial elements function equally in Klee's work, delighting the eye and amusing the mind.

42. RED BALLOON. 1922
(Roter Ballon)
Oil (and oil transfer drawing?) on chalk-primed linen
gauze mounted on board, 12½ × 12¼ in.
(31.7 × 31.1 cm.)
Acquired 1948

A red balloon is suspended in space over a cityscape
that is simultaneously fantastic and intelligible. The
imaginary architectures and illusionary perspectives
that were among Klee's major themes are found in this
painting of 1922. The same geometric structure and
diaphanous color appear in another picture of the same
year, *Little Fir-Tree Painting* (Collection Kunstmu-
scum Basel). Although in earlier works the artist made
specific references to houses through details such as
windows and slanted roofs, here such images are reduced to a minimum. The resulting schematic render-
ing anticipates the purely abstract compositions of colored rectangles that Klee began in 1923.

The balloon is a recurrent motif in Klee's work: *The
Balloon* (1926) and *Balloon over Town* (1928) are other
examples of its use. In the Guggenheim's picture, Klee
took advantage of the weave of the chalk-primed linen
gauze and the way this support absorbed the paint to
create an enchanting pictorial space.

43. NEW HARMONY. 1936
(Neue Harmonie)
Oil on canvas, 36⅞ × 26⅛ in. (93.6 × 66.3 cm.)
Acquired 1971

New Harmony is one of only twenty-five works Klee
executed in 1936 when he was very ill. One of a series
of paintings called "magic squares," it contains the
two-dimensional colored rectangles that first appeared
in his art in 1923. Essentially it looks back to Klee's
color theory of the 1920s and even the title belongs with
those works he designated "Architecture, Harmony,
and Sound." While related to *Ancient Sound*, 1925
(Collection Kunstmuseum Basel), *New Harmony* is
based on brighter colors, over a dark underpainting,
which are firmly anchored into a more rigorous grid
pattern and now arranged according to the principle of
inverted bilateral symmetry. Like so many of his other
pictures it reflects the artist's study of musical harmony.

Amedeo Modigliani

1884–1920. Amedeo Modigliani was born on July 12, 1884, in Leghorn, Italy. The serious illnesses he suffered during his childhood (typhus and tuberculosis among them) persisted throughout his life. At the age of fourteen he began to study painting. He first experimented with sculpture during the summer of 1902 and the following year attended the Istituto di Belle Arti in Venice. Early in 1906 Modigliani went to Paris, where he settled in Montmartre and attended the Académie Colarossi. His early work was influenced by Toulouse-Lautrec, Théophile-Alexandre Steinlen, Gauguin, and Cézanne. In the autumn of 1907 he met his first patron, Dr. Paul Alexandre, who purchased works from him before World War I. Modigliani exhibited in the Salon d'Automne in 1907 and 1912 and in the Salon des Indépendants in 1908, 1910, and 1911.

In 1909 Modigliani met Brancusi when both artists lived in Montparnasse. From 1909 to 1915 the Italian concentrated on sculpture but he also drew and painted to a certain extent. The majority of his paintings, however, date from 1916 to 1919. Modigliani's circle of friends first consisted of Max Jacob, Lipchitz, and the Portuguese sculptor Amedeo de Suza Cardoso and later included Chaim Soutine, Maurice Utrillo, Jules Pascin, Tsugouharu Foujita, Moïse Kisling, and the Sitwells. His dealers were Paul Guillaume (1914 to 1916) and Leopold Zborowski (from 1917 onward). The only one-man show given the artist during his lifetime took place at the Galerie Berthe Weill in December 1917.

In March 1917 Modigliani met Jeanne Hébuterne, who became his companion and model. From March or April 1918 until May 31, 1919, they lived in the south of France, in both Nice and Cagnes. Modigliani died in Paris on January 24, 1920.

50. Nude. 1917
(Nu)
Oil on canvas, 28¾ × 45⅞ in. (73 × 116.7 cm.)
Gift, Solomon R. Guggenheim, 1941

Modigliani has shown the reclining female nude asleep: thus, she does not gaze provocatively at the spectator as in many of his other paintings of the subject. Between 1916 and 1919 he painted approximately twenty-six female nudes. When a group of these canvases (perhaps including the Guggenheim's painting) was shown at the Galerie Berthe Weill in December 1917, the police found them to be obscene and closed the exhibition.

Modigliani's sleeping figure appears self-contained, sensuous, and unaware of the viewer. The warm flesh-color of her body is set off on one side by the dark color of the background and on the other by the white drapery. Her head is described in a rather stylized manner contrasting with the full, naturalistic modeling of her torso.

COLORPLATES

Gleizes • Gris • Picabia • Duchamp • Kupka • Delaunay • Kirchner • Nolde •
Kokoschka • Schiele • Jawlensky • Kandinsky • Marc • Klee • Feininger •
Severini • Chagall • Brancusi • Modigliani

25. ALBERT GLEIZES *Brooklyn Bridge.* 1915

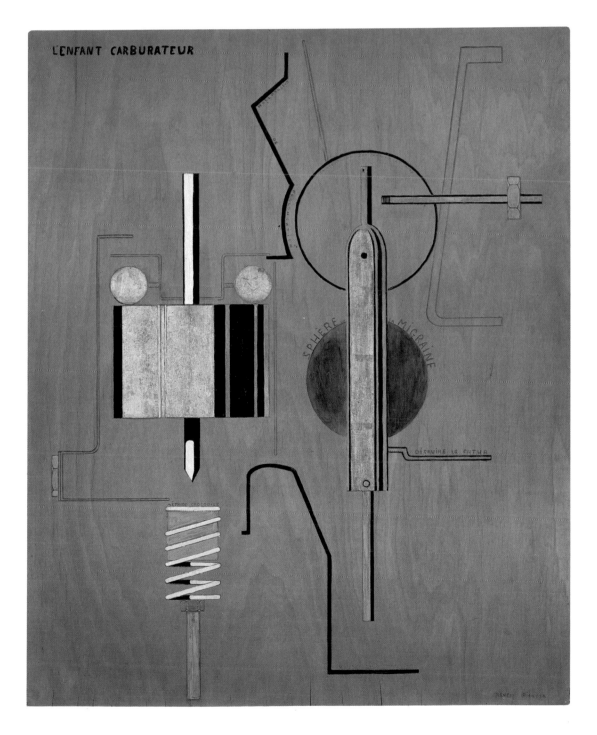

31. ROBERT DELAUNAY *Simultaneous Windows (2nd Motif, 1st Part).* 1912

33. EMIL NOLDE *Young Horses.* 1916

34. OSKAR KOKOSCHKA *Knight Errant.* 1915

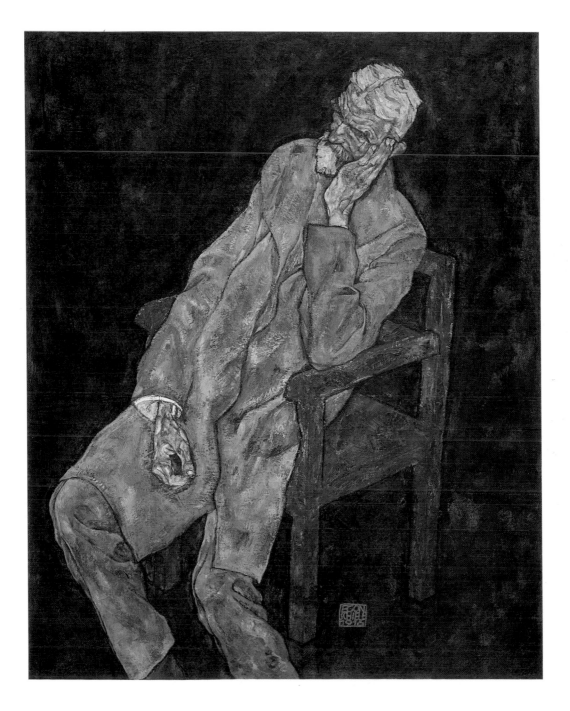

36. ALEXEJ JAWLENSKY *Helene with Colored Turban.* 1910

38. VASILY KANDINSKY *Painting with White Border.* 1913

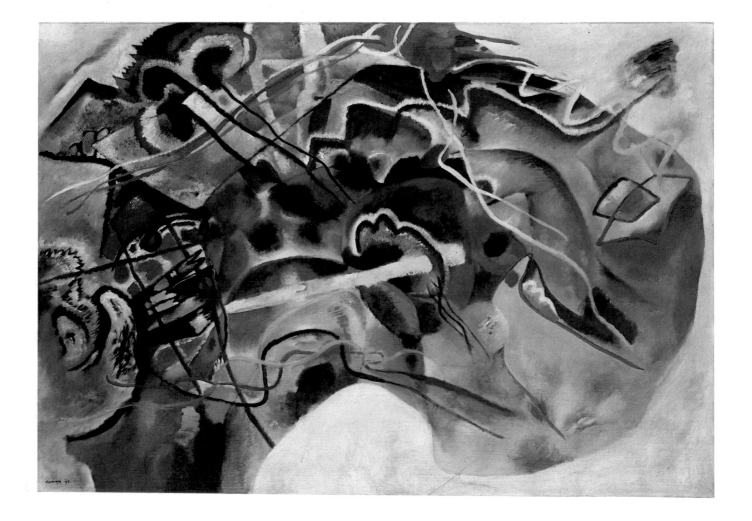

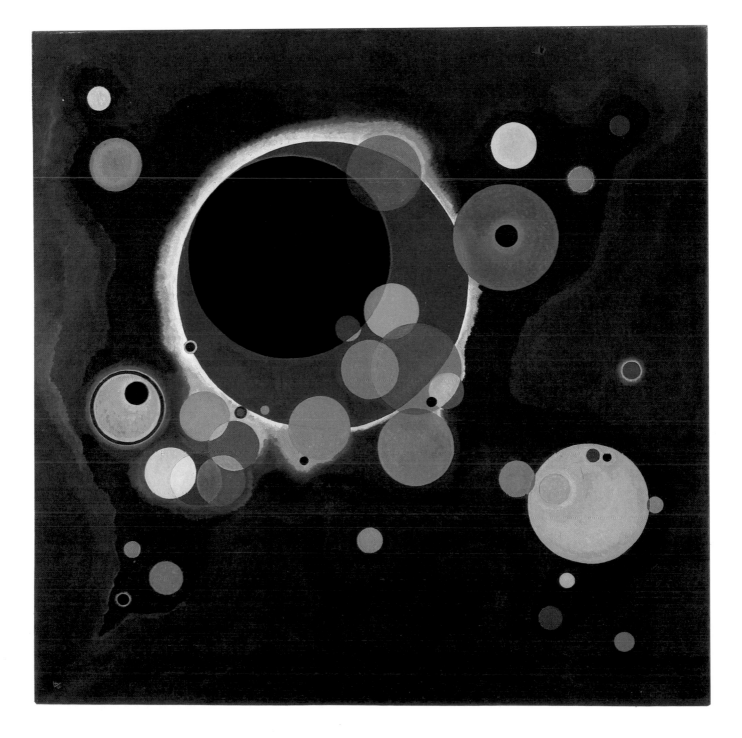

40. FRANZ MARC *Yellow Cow.* 1911

41. PAUL KLEE *The Bavarian Don Giovanni.* 1919

42. PAUL KLEE *Red Balloon.* 1922

43. PAUL KLEE *New Harmony.* 1936

44. LYONEL FEININGER *Gelmeroda IV.* 1915

COMMENTARIES

Archipenko • Lipchitz • Larionov • Malevich • Popova • Mondrian • Van Doesburg • Gabo • Pevsner •
Moholy-Nagy • Schwitters • Ernst • Arp • Miró • Giacometti • Beckmann • Moore • Matta • Tamayo •
Dubuffet • Bacon • Jorn • Ipoustéguy • Hamilton • Calder • Albers • Hofmann • Lindner • Cornell

ALEXANDER ARCHIPENKO 1887–1964. Alexander Archipenko was born on May 30, 1887, in Kiev, Russia. He
studied painting and sculpture at art school in Kiev, but was expelled in 1905 for criticizing his teachers' acade-
micism. During this time he was impressed by the Byzantine icons, frescoes, and mosaics of Kiev. After a sojourn
in Moscow Archipenko moved to Paris in 1908 and studied independently at the Louvre. In 1910 he began exhibiting
at the Salon des Indépendants, Paris, and the following year showed for the first time at the Salon d'Automne.

In 1912 Archipenko was given his first one-man show in Germany at the Folkwang Museum in Hagen. That
same year in Paris he opened the first of his many art schools, joined the Section d'Or group, which included
Picasso, Braque, Léger, and Duchamp among others, and produced his first painted reliefs, the *Sculpto-Peintures*.
Archipenko made his first prints and exhibited at the Armory Show in New York in 1913. During the war years the
artist resided in Cimiez, a suburb of Nice. From 1919 to 1921 he traveled to Geneva, Zürich, Paris, London,
Brussels, Athens, and other European cities to exhibit his work. Archipenko's first one-man show in the United
States was held at the Société Anonyme in New York in 1921.

In 1923 he moved from Berlin to the United States, where, over the years, he opened art schools in various cities.
In 1924 Archipenko invented his first kinetic work, *Archipentura*. For the next thirty years he taught in the United
States at art schools and universities. He became a United States citizen in 1928. Most of Archipenko's work in
German museums was confiscated by the Nazis in their 1937 purge of *Entartete Kunst* (degenerate art). In 1947 he
produced the first of his sculptures to be illuminated from within. In 1955 he began work on the book *Archipenko:
Fifty Creative Years 1908–1958*, published in 1960. The artist died on February 25, 1964, in New York.

51. MÉDRANO II. 1913

Painted tin, wood, glass, and painted oilcloth, 49⅞
× 20¼ × 12½ in. (126.6 × 51.5 × 31.7 cm.)
Acquired 1956

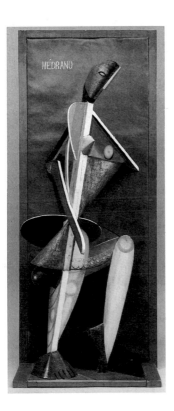

The inscription *"MÉDRANO"* refers to the famous circus of that name in
boulevard Rochechouart in Paris which many artists frequented. In 1912, a
year before this relief was done, Archipenko had created *Médrano I* (now
destroyed), his first multi-material construction. Made from wood, glass,
sheet metal, and found objects, it represented a juggler. In *Médrano II* the
figure of the dancer is positioned on a base in front of a framed rectangular
background that is painted red. Thus, the artist controls the spectator's view
of the sculpture. He has assembled carefully selected and precisely crafted
materials: reflective metal surfaces in the face and torso, glass for the skirt,
and various pieces of painted wood. He has organized the volumes along a
slightly tipped, vertical axis and defined the figure by means of projecting
planes. A curved element of wood painted blue determines the angle of the
dancer's shoulders, a cylindrical tin form and a circle painted on glass in-
dicate her breasts, a projecting wood disc describes the rotation of her hips,
and the thrust of her extended leg is parallel to the major vertical axis.

JACQUES LIPCHITZ 1891–1973. Chaim Jacob Lipschitz was born on August 22, 1891, in Druskieniki, Lithuania. At the age of eighteen he moved to Paris, where he attended the Ecole des Beaux-Arts and the Académie Julian and soon met Picasso, Gris, and Braque. In 1912 he began exhibiting at the Salon de la Société Nationale des Beaux-Arts and the Salon d'Automne. Lipchitz's first one-man show was held at Léonce Rosenberg's Galerie l'Effort Moderne in Paris in 1920. Two years later he executed five bas-reliefs for The Barnes Foundation in Merion, Pennsylvania. In 1924 the artist became a French citizen and the following year moved to Boulogne-sur-Seine. He received a commission from the Vicomte Charles de Noailles in 1927 for what would become one of his most famous sculptures, *Joy of Life.*

Lipchitz's first important retrospective took place at Jeanne Bucher's Galerie de la Renaissance in Paris in 1930. The Brummer Gallery in New York hosted his first large show in the United States in 1935. In 1941 Lipchitz fled Paris for New York, where he began exhibiting regularly at the Buchholz Gallery (later the Curt Valentin Gallery). He settled in Hastings-on-Hudson, New York, in 1947. In 1954 a Lipchitz retrospective traveled from The Museum of Modern Art in New York to the Walker Art Center in Minneapolis and The Cleveland Museum of Art. In 1958 Lipchitz became a United States citizen. He visited Israel for the first time in 1963. From 1964 to 1966 Lipchitz showed annually at the Marlborough-Gerson Gallery in New York. Beginning in 1963 he spent several months of each year casting in Pietrasanta, Italy.

From 1970 until 1973 he worked on large-scale commissions for the Municipal Plaza in Philadelphia, Columbia University in New York, and the Hadassah Medical Center near Jerusalem. These projects were completed after Lipchitz's death by his wife, Yulla. In 1972 the artist's autobiography was published on the occasion of an exhibition of his sculpture at The Metropolitan Museum of Art in New York. Lipchitz died on May 26, 1973, on Capri, and was buried in Jerusalem.

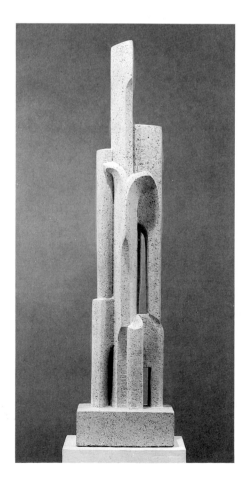

52. STANDING PERSONAGE. 1916
(Personnage debout)
Limestone, 42½ in. (108 cm.) high
Acquired 1958

More than fifty years after its execution, Lipchitz stated that *Standing Personage* "was completely realized in the round as a three-dimensional object existing in three-dimensional space. Thus, when it is seen in a photograph, it is impossible to understand the work fully. The vertical architectural basis of the structure is apparent. . . . While this sculpture is in one sense an architectural construction, it is also clearly a figure or figures. The V-shaped curves rising from the sharp vertical in the upper central area reiterate the eyebrows and nose of the slightly earlier head, and the angled elements at the bottom can be either the buttresses supporting a Gothic vault or the legs of a seated figure." (J. Lipchitz with H. H. Arnason, *My Life in Sculpture,* New York, 1972, p. 37.)

In addition to the Guggenheim's version, which was carved from a limestone block, Lipchitz made a plaster of similar dimensions about 1916 (Collection Musée National d'Art Moderne, Paris) that was cast in bronze.

MIKHAIL LARIONOV

1881–1964. Mikhail Federovich Larionov was born on May 22, 1881, at Tiraspol in Bessarabia, Russia. From 1898 to 1908 he studied at the Moscow School of Painting, Sculpture, and Architecture, where he met Natalia Goncharova; the two lived and worked together until her death in 1962. In 1906 he visited Paris with Sergei Diaghilev, who included Larionov's work in the exhibition of Russian artists at the Salon d'Automne of that year. In 1907 the artist abandoned the Impressionism of his previous work for a Neo-Primitive style inspired by Russian folk art. With the Burliuk brothers and others he formed the Blue Rose group, under whose auspices the review *The Golden Fleece* was published. The first Golden Fleece exhibition of 1908 in Moscow introduced many modern French masters to the Russian public. Larionov also organized the avant-garde "Link" and "Donkey's Tail" exhibitions of 1908 and 1912 respectively and founded the Jack of Diamonds group in 1910.

In 1911 he developed a personal abstract style which would later be known as Rayonism. An amalgam of Cubism and Italian Futurism, with an emphasis on dynamic, linear light rays, Rayonism received its first public showing at the "Target" exhibition of 1913. That same year Larionov's Rayonist Manifesto was published in Moscow. The artist also participated in the Erster Deutscher Herbstsalon (First German Autumn Salon) at the gallery of Der Sturm in Berlin in 1913, and the following year organized the exhibition "No. 4" in Moscow. In May 1914 Larionov and Goncharova accompanied Diaghilev's Ballets Russes to Paris; there Larionov associated with Apollinaire. He returned to Russia in July upon the outbreak of World War I and served at the front until his demobilization for health reasons. He then rejoined Diaghilev in Switzerland and devoted himself almost exclusively to designing sets and costumes for the Ballets Russes. After Diaghilev died in 1929, Larionov organized a retrospective of maquettes, costumes, and decor for his ballets at the Galerie Billiet in Paris in 1930, at which time he published *Les Ballets Russes de Diaghilev* with Goncharova and Pierre Vorms.

In 1938 Larionov became a French citizen. He and Goncharova were given a number of joint exhibitions throughout their careers, among them retrospectives in Paris at the Galerie des Deux-Iles in 1948, the Galerie de l'Institut in 1952, and the Musée National d'Art Moderne in 1963. A one-man exhibition of Larionov's work was held in 1956 at the Galerie de l'Institut. He died on May 10, 1964, at Fontenay-aux-Roses.

53. GLASS. 1912
(Steklo; Le Verre)
Oil on canvas, 41 × 38¼ in. (104.1 × 97.1 cm.)
Acquired 1953

Larionov was not only a painter but an organizer of exhibitions and the author of the Rayonist Manifesto. He considered *Glass* to have been his first Rayonist picture: in it Larionov has depicted five tumblers, a goblet, and two bottles so that their essential forms are retained; lines then represent rays reflected from the objects. As early as 1913 it was observed that Larionov was not painting a still life but "simply 'glass' as a universal condition of glass with all its manifestations and properties—fragility, ease in breaking, sharpness, transparency, brittleness, ability to make sounds, i.e. the sum of all the sensations, obtainable from glass. . . ." (Translation from A. Z. Rudenstine, *The Guggenheim Museum Collection: Paintings 1880–1945,* New York, 1976, p. 447.)

KAZIMIR MALEVICH 1878–1935. Kazimir Severinovich Malevich was born on February 26, 1878, near Kiev, Russia. He studied at the Moscow School of Painting, Sculpture, and Architecture in 1903. During the early years of his career he experimented with various modernist styles and participated in avant-garde exhibitions, among them those of the Moscow Association of Artists, which included Kandinsky and Larionov, and the 1910 Jack of Diamonds show in Moscow. Malevich showed his Neo-Primitivist paintings of peasants at the "Donkey's Tail" exhibition in 1912. In 1913, with the composer M. V. Matyushin and the writer Alexej Kruchyonykh, he drafted a manifesto for the First Futurist Congress. That same year Malevich designed the sets and costumes for Matyushin's and Kruchyonykh's opera *Victory over the Sun*. He showed at the Salon des Indépendants, Paris, in 1914.

At the "Last Futurist Exhibition of Pictures: 0.10," held in Petrograd in 1915, Malevich introduced his nonobjective, geometric Suprematist paintings. In 1919 he began to explore the three-dimensional applications of Suprematism in architectural models. Following the Bolshevik Revolution, Malevich and other advanced artists were encouraged by the Soviet government. A state exhibition in Moscow in 1919 focused on Suprematism and other nonobjective styles, and later that year Malevich was given a retrospective in Moscow. Also in 1919, at the invitation of Chagall, he began teaching at the Vitebsk Academy, where, because of ideological differences, he soon replaced Chagall as director. Malevich's students at Vitebsk formed the Suprematist group Unovis. From 1922 to 1927 he taught at the Institute for Artistic Culture in Petrograd and between 1924 and 1926 he worked primarily on architectural models with his students. He was active also as a theoretician and writer.

Malevich traveled with an exhibition of his paintings to Warsaw and Berlin in 1927. In Germany he met Arp, Kurt Schwitters, Naum Gabo, and Le Corbusier and visited the Bauhaus, where he met Walter Gropius. Because of his connections with German artists, Malevich was arrested in 1930 and many of his manuscripts were destroyed. In his final period he painted in a representational style. Malevich died in Leningrad on May 15, 1935.

54. MORNING IN THE VILLAGE AFTER SNOWSTORM. 1912

(Utro posle v'yugi v derevne)
Oil on canvas, 31¾ × 31⅞ in. (80.7 × 80.8 cm.)
Acquired 1952

Morning in the Village After Snowstorm belongs with Malevich's peasant pictures of 1911–12 (for example, *In the Fields, The Reaper, Woodcutter,* and *Taking in the Rye*), which show solid, compact figures tending to daily chores. In the Guggenheim's painting Malevich has emphasized volume through the shapes of the cylinder, sphere, and cone. Even the snowdrifts have been stylized into geometric forms. The colors are predominantly white, red, and blue with an almost metallic and decidedly non-naturalistic cast. The geometric and tubular forms suggest those of Léger, whose work Malevich could have known from the Jack of Diamonds exhibition in Moscow in February 1912 or through reproductions.

LIUBOV POPOVA 1889–1924. Liubov Sergeevna Popova was born near Moscow on April 24, 1889. After graduating from high school in Yalta, she studied in Moscow at the Arsenieva Gymnasium in 1907–8 and at the same time attended the studios of Stanislav Zhukovsky and Konstantin Yuon. In the course of her travels in 1909–10 she saw Mikhail Vrubel's work in Kiev, ancient Russian churches in Pskov and Novgorod, and early Renaissance art in Italy. In 1912 Popova worked at The Tower, a Moscow studio, with Vladimir Tatlin and other artists. That winter she visited Paris, where she worked in the studios of the Cubist painters Le Fauconnier and Metzinger. In 1913 Popova returned to Russia but the following year she journeyed again to France and to Italy, where she gained familiarity with Futurism.

In her work of 1912 to 1915 Popova was concerned with Cubist form and the representation of movement; after 1915 her nonrepresentational style revealed the influence of icon painting. She participated in many exhibitions of advanced art in Russia during this period: the Jack of Diamonds shows of 1914 and 1916 in Moscow; "Tramway V: First Futurist Exhibition of Paintings" and "Last Futurist Exhibition of Pictures: 0.10," both in 1915 in Petrograd; "The Store" in 1916, "Fifth State Exhibition: From Impressionism to Nonobjective Art" in 1918–19, and "Tenth State Exhibition: Nonobjective Creation and Suprematism" in 1919, all in Moscow. In 1916 Popova joined the Supremus group, which was organized by Malevich. She taught at Svomas (Free State Art Studios) and Vkhutemas (Higher State Art-Technical Institute) from 1918 onward and was a member of Inkhuk (Institute of Painterly Culture) from 1920 to 1923.

The artist participated in the "5 × 5 = 25" exhibition in Moscow in 1921 and in the Erste Russische Kunstausstellung (First Russian Art Exhibition), held under the auspices of the Russian government in Berlin in 1922. In 1921 Popova turned away from studio painting to execute utilitarian Productivist art: she designed textiles, dresses, books, porcelain, costumes, and theater sets (the latter for Vsevolod Meierkhold's productions of Fernand Crommelynk's *The Magnanimous Cuckold,* 1922, and Sergei Tretiakov's *Earth in Turmoil,* 1923). Popova died in Moscow on May 25, 1924, at the age of thirty-five.

55. LANDSCAPE. 1914–15
Oil on canvas, 41¾ × 27⅜ in. (106 × 69.5 cm.)
Gift, George Costakis, 1981

Like other Russian artists, Popova went to Paris, where she became familiar with the Cubists, and to Italy, where she saw the work of the Futurists. Her *Landscape* clearly belongs within the Cubo-Futurist style and was painted just before her breakthrough to nonobjective art. In marked contrast to the practice of the French Cubists, Popova restricts her bright, bold colors to specific areas of the painting. Color defines compositional elements: purple-blue in the sky, green in the grass, brown for the earth, and gray-blue for the buildings. Color zones remain discrete and the geometrical forms, which are modeled with distinctive white highlights, retain their three-dimensionality. Forms, unlike those in Cubist paintings, appear volumetric rather than fragmented. Popova's composition is dynamic and dominated by a central foreground configuration.

PIET MONDRIAN

1872–1944. Piet Mondrian was born Pieter Cornelis Mondriaan, Jr., on March 7, 1872, in Amersfoort, the Netherlands. He studied at the Rijksakademie van Beeldende Kunsten, Amsterdam, from 1892 to 1897. Until 1908, when he began to take annual trips to Domburg in Zeeland, Mondrian's work was naturalistic—incorporating successive influences of academic landscape and still-life painting, Dutch Impressionism, and Symbolism. In 1909 a major exhibition of his work (with that of C. R. H. Spoor and Jan Sluyters) was held at the Stedelijk Museum, Amsterdam, and that same year he joined the Theosophic Society. In 1909–10 he experimented with Pointillism and by 1911 had begun to work in a Cubist mode. After seeing original Cubist works by Braque and Picasso at the first Moderne Kunstkring exhibition in 1911 in Amsterdam, Mondrian decided to move to Paris. In Paris from 1912 to 1914 he began to develop an independent abstract style.

Mondrian was visiting the Netherlands when World War I broke out, preventing his return to Paris. During the war years in Holland he further reduced his colors and geometric shapes and formulated his nonobjective Neo-Plastic style. In 1917 Mondrian became one of the founders of De Stijl. This group, which included Van Doesburg and Vantongerloo, extended the principles of abstraction and simplification beyond painting and sculpture to include architecture and graphic and industrial design as well. Mondrian's essays on abstract art were published in the periodical *De Stijl*. In July 1919 he returned to Paris; there he exhibited with De Stijl in 1923 but withdrew from the group after Van Doesburg reintroduced diagonal elements into his work about 1925. In 1930 Mondrian showed with the Cercle et Carré (Circle and Square) artists and in 1931 joined the Abstraction-Création group.

World War II forced Mondrian to move to London in 1938 and then to settle in New York in October 1940. In New York he joined the American Abstract Artists and continued to publish texts on Neo-Plasticism. His late style evolved significantly in response to the city. In 1942 his first one-man show took place at the Valentine Gallery, New York. Mondrian died on February 1, 1944, in New York. In 1971 The Solomon R. Guggenheim Museum organized a centennial exhibition of his work.

56. COMPOSITION 1916. 1916
Oil on canvas with wood strip at bottom edge, 46⅞ × 29⅝ in. (119 × 75.1 cm.)
Acquired 1949

During the years 1915 and 1916 Mondrian began to abandon subjects derived from observable reality such as trees, dunes, the sea, and buildings and concentrated on purely nonobjective compositions. *Composition 1916,* which is his only known work dated 1916, evolved from a series of charcoal sketches of the church facade at Domburg on the coast of Dutch Zeeland. The artist designed a strip frame (now lost) in which the canvas was meant to be seen. His selection of an ocher, blue, and rose palette with a gray ground appears to be a movement in the direction of the primary colors: yellow, blue, and red.

Mondrian's work of the war years in Holland is characterized by a breakdown of his familiar grid into an empirically improvised cross and line pattern, resulting in a punctuated yet uninterrupted flow of space. Although the black lines are limited to horizontals and verticals, the areas of color are applied in diagonal cadence. Thus, as was his avowed practice, Mondrian provoked an opposition or duality of pictorial elements, to be resolved through a dynamic balance or "plastic equivalence."

57. COMPOSITION 2. 1922
(Tableau 2)
Oil on canvas, 21⅞ × 21⅛ in. (55.6 × 53.4 cm.)
Acquired 1951

By 1921 Mondrian had reduced his palette to the three primary colors, black, and gray-white. Organizing his pictures according to a grid of exclusively horizontal and vertical black lines, he structured his compositions around a dominant gray-white square or rectangle framed by black lines and he limited his color to smaller marginal zones. The year 1922 was one of simplification of both color and line relationships, anticipating the artist's later and generally more austere work.

The format of *Composition 2* is almost square, slightly higher than it is wide. The central area is almost square in opposite proportion, slightly wider than high. The gray background begins to occur frequently about 1921–22 and continues throughout the 1920s, when Mondrian lived in Paris. He mixed small amounts of primary color pigment into the noncolor zones, thus creating different kinds of chromatic relationships, based not on white but on off-white variants.

A common De Stijl device encountered here is the discontinuation of lines before they reach the edge of the canvas. According to the painter Vantongerloo, "the practice originated from a fear that the abstract composition would lose its organic compactness if all lines were carried through to the edge of the composition, bisecting it completely." (R. P. Welsh, *Piet Mondrian 1872–1944,* exh. cat., Toronto, 1966, p. 178.) Mondrian was to abandon this pictorial principle by the late 1920s.

58. COMPOSITION I A. 1930
Oil on canvas (lozenge), 29⅝ × 29⅝ in. (75.2 × 75.2 cm.)
Acquired 1971

About 1930 to 1933 Mondrian eliminated color in many of his compositions, so that the white plane of the canvas is crossed by a few black lines. These are works of utmost simplicity in which the placement and varying thickness of lines determine the painting's harmony and rhythm.

The lozenge shape of *Composition 1 A* results from rotating a square forty-five degrees. Mondrian first used this format in 1918, but the majority of his diamond-shaped canvases date from 1925–26. The integrity of the rectilinear design survives even when superimposed on and truncated by the contrasting shape of the lozenge. The inherent unity of the square transcends the limits of the canvas and completes itself outside the picture plane. This extension into surrounding space is seen to an even greater degree in *Composition with Yellow Lines,* 1933 (Collection Gemeentemuseum, The Hague), where none of the lines intersect within the canvas.

THEO VAN DOESBURG 1883–1931. Christian Emil Marie Küpper, who adopted the pseudonym Theo van Doesburg, was born in Utrecht, the Netherlands, on August 30, 1883. His first exhibition of paintings was held in 1908
in The Hague. From 1911 to 1913 he wrote poetry and established himself as an art critic; from 1914 to 1916 he
served in the Dutch army, after which time he settled in Leiden and began his collaboration with the architects
J. J. P. Oud and Jan Wils. In 1917 they founded the group De Stijl and the periodical of the same name; other
original members were Mondrian, Vantongerloo, Bart van der Leck, and Vilmos Huszár. Van Doesburg executed
decorations for Oud's De Vonk project in Noordwijkerhout in 1917.

In 1920 he resumed his writing, using the pen names I. K. Bonset and later Aldo Camini. Van Doesburg visited
Berlin and Weimar in 1921 and the following year taught at the Weimar Bauhaus, where he associated with Mies
van der Rohe, Le Corbusier, Raoul Hausmann, and Hans Richter. He was interested in Dada at this time and
worked with Schwitters as well as Arp, Tristan Tzara, and others on the review *Mécano* in 1922. Exhibitions of
the architectural designs of Van Doesburg, Cor van Eesteren, and Gerrit Rietveld were held in Paris in 1923 at
Léonce Rosenberg's Galerie l'Effort Moderne and in 1924 at the Ecole Spéciale d'Architecture.

The Landesmuseum of Weimar presented a one-man show of Van Doesburg's work in 1924. That same year he
lectured on modern literature in Prague, Vienna, and Hannover, and the Bauhaus published his *Grundbegriffe der
neuen gestaltenden Kunst (Principles of Neo-Plastic Art)*. A new phase of De Stijl was declared by Van Doesburg
in his manifesto of Elementarism, published in 1926. During that year he collaborated with Arp and Sophie Taeuber-
Arp on the decoration of the restaurant-cabaret L'Aubette in Strasbourg. Van Doesburg returned to Paris in 1929
and began working on a house at Meudon-Val-Fleury with Van Eesteren. Also in 1929 he published the first issue
of *Art Concret*, the organ of the Paris-based group of the same name. Van Doesburg was the moving force behind
the formation of the Abstraction-Création group in Paris. The artist died on March 7, 1931, in Davos, Switzerland.

59. COMPOSITION XI. 1918
Oil on canvas mounted in artist's painted frame,
sight, 22⅜ × 39⅞ in. (56.9 × 101.3 cm.)
Acquired 1954

When the painters of the De Stijl movement formed a
group in the spring of 1917, the similar conclusions each
had come to over a period of individual investigation
reinforced their unity and, by 1918, they arrived at a
reduction of form and color to a pure, elemental level.
Van Doesburg's paintings of this time demonstrate a
synthesis of Mondrian's and Van der Leck's work. As
Mondrian had often done, Van Doesburg designed a
painted frame in which this picture was meant to be—
and indeed is—seen.

Composition XI is one of Van Doesburg's abstract
geometric compositions of rectangular color planes
floating on the surface of the canvas. Color is limited
to subdued red, yellow, and blue on an off-white
ground: a variation on his more common palette of pri-
maries on white. While a representational origin can
be found for most of these abstract works, none has
come to light for the Guggenheim's picture. In his exploration of the relationship between line, plane, and
color, Van Doesburg has arranged the planes over the
background to achieve balance through an intuitive
rather than a systematic method of placement.

NAUM GABO
1890–1977. Naum Neemia Pevsner was born on August 5, 1890, in Briansk, Russia. From 1910 to 1911 he studied medicine, science, and art history at the University in Munich. In 1913 and 1914 he visited Paris, where he saw the work of Gleizes, Metzinger, Léger, and Robert Delaunay. During World War I he lived in Oslo with his brother Antoine Pevsner. He executed his first construction in 1915 and signed it "Gabo."

In 1917 Gabo settled in Moscow, where he associated with Tatlin, Malevich, and Alexander Rodchenko. He and Pevsner published their *Realistic Manifesto* in 1920. In 1922 they participated in the Erste Russische Kunstausstellung (First Russian Art Exhibition) at the Galerie van Diemen in Berlin. Gabo lived in Berlin for the next decade. The exhibition "Constructivistes russes: Gabo et Pevsner" was held at the Galerie Percier in Paris in 1924. Gabo was given his first one-man show in 1930 at the Kestner-Gesellschaft in Hannover. In 1932 the artist left Germany for Paris, where he became a leading member of the Abstraction-Création group. He moved to England in 1936.

Gabo visited the United States for the first time in 1938, when his sculpture was shown at the Wadsworth Atheneum in Hartford, the Julien Levy Gallery in New York, and Vassar College in Poughkeepsie. In 1944 in London he worked with the critic Herbert Read in the Design Research Unit, which promoted cooperation between artists and industry. Gabo moved to the United States in 1946 and two years later shared an exhibition with Pevsner at The Museum of Modern Art in New York. In 1952 he became a United States citizen and from 1953 to 1954 taught at the Harvard University Graduate School of Architecture. During the mid-1950s the artist worked on commissions for the De Bijenkorf building in Rotterdam and for the United States Rubber Company at Rockefeller Center in New York. In 1973 he received a sculpture commission from the Nationalgalerie of Berlin. The Tate Gallery in London presented a major exhibition of his work in 1976. Gabo died on August 23, 1977, in Middlebury, Connecticut.

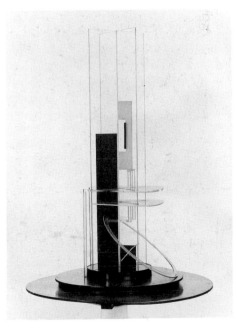

60. COLUMN. c. 1923. Reconstructed in 1937
Perspex, wood, metal, and glass, 41½ × 29 × 29 in.
(105.3 × 73.6 × 73.6 cm.)
Acquired 1955

Gabo considered *Column* a work "of great importance not only to my own development, but it can be historically proved that it is a cornerstone in the whole development of contemporary architecture." (Letter to Bartlett H. Hayes, Jr., Director, Addison Gallery of American Art, Mar. 13, 1949.) He emphasized that the *Column* was the culmination of his "search for an image which would fuse the sculptural element with the architectural element into one unit." (H. Read and L. Martin, *Gabo: Constructions, Sculpture, Paintings, Drawings, Engravings*, Cambridge, Mass., 1957, opp. pl. 26.) The vertical elements are rectangular constructions within parabolas that are determined by the dimensions of the bases.

There are several versions of the column: a five-inch celluloid model (Collection Tate Gallery, London), three versions approximately eleven inches high (Collections Yale University Art Gallery, New Haven; Sir Leslie Martin; and Estate of the artist), and two monumental versions over six feet high, both executed in 1975 (Collections Louisiana Museum, Humlebaek, Denmark, and Estate of the artist). It is very difficult to place these sculptures in sequence.

ANTOINE PEVSNER

1884–1962. Antoine Pevsner was born on January 18, 1884, in Orel, Russia. After leaving the Academy of Fine Arts in St. Petersburg in 1911, he traveled to Paris, where he saw the work of Robert Delaunay, Gleizes, Metzinger, and Léger. On a second visit to Paris in 1913 he met Modigliani and Archipenko, who encouraged his interest in Cubism. Pevsner spent the war years 1915 to 1917 in Oslo with his brother Naum Gabo. On his return to Russia in 1917 Pevsner began teaching at the Moscow Academy of Fine Arts with Kandinsky and Malevich.

In 1920 he and Gabo published the *Realistic Manifesto*. Their work was included in the Erste Russische Kunstausstellung (First Russian Art Exhibition) at the Galerie van Diemen in Berlin in 1922. The following year Pevsner visited Berlin, where he met Duchamp and Katherine Dreier. He then traveled on to Paris; he settled permanently in that city and in 1930 became a French citizen. His work was included in an exhibition at the Little Review Gallery in New York in 1926. He and Gabo designed sets for the ballet *La Chatte*, produced by Sergei Diaghilev in 1927. The two brothers were also leaders of the Constructivist members of the Abstraction-Création group.

During the 1930s Pevsner's work was shown in Amsterdam, Basel, London, New York, and Chicago. In 1946 he, Gleizes, Herbin, and others formed the group Réalités Nouvelles; their first exhibition was held at the Salon des Réalités Nouvelles in Paris in 1946. That same year Pevsner's first one-man show opened at the Galerie René Drouin in Paris. The Museum of Modern Art in New York presented a Gabo-Pevsner exhibition in 1948, and in 1952 Pevsner participated in the "Chefs-d'oeuvre du XXᵉ siècle" exhibition at the Musée National d'Art Moderne in Paris. The same museum organized a one-man exhibition of his work in 1957. In 1958 he was represented in the French Pavilion at the Venice Biennale. Pevsner died in Paris on April 12, 1962.

61. TWINNED COLUMN. 1947
(Colonne jumelée)
Bronze, 40½ in. (102.9 cm.) high
Acquired 1954

Like his brother Gabo, Pevsner experimented with the possibilities of new materials and techniques in his sculpture. In addition to working in plastics, he created many constructions from bronze, brass, and tin. Frequently he incorporated more than one substance in a single sculpture to provide color, surface texture, and patterning of light and shadow. In *Twinned Column* bronze rods reminiscent of the nylon filaments Gabo used are joined together to form linear configurations. Both *Twinned Column* and *Developable Column of Victory* from the previous year are freestanding sculptures with strong central axes and silhouettes that change when seen from different points of view. The bold symmetry of both compositions and the contrast between solid and void are characteristic of Pevsner's work.

122

LÁSZLÓ MOHOLY-NAGY

1895–1946. László Moholy-Nagy was born on July 20, 1895, in Bacsbarsod, Hungary. In 1913 he began law studies at the University of Budapest but interrupted them the following year to serve in the Austro-Hungarian army. While recovering from a wound in 1917, he founded the artists' group MA (today) with Ludwig Kassak and others in Szeged, Hungary, and started a literary magazine called *Jelenkor* (the present). After receiving his law degree, Moholy-Nagy moved to Vienna in 1919, where he collaborated on the MA periodical *Horizont*. He traveled to Berlin in 1920 and began making "photograms" and Dada collages.

During the early 1920s Moholy-Nagy contributed to several important art periodicals and coedited with Kassak *Das Buch neuer Künstler*, a volume of poetry and essays on art. In 1921 he met El Lissitzky in Germany and traveled to Paris for the first time. His first one-man exhibition was organized by Herwarth Walden at Der Sturm in Berlin in 1922. During this period Moholy-Nagy was a seminal figure in the development of Constructivism. While teaching at the Bauhaus in Weimar in 1923, he became involved in stage and book design and with Walter Gropius edited and designed the Bauhausbücher series published by the school. In 1926 he began to experiment with unconventional materials such as aluminum and bakelite. Moholy-Nagy moved with the Bauhaus to Dessau in 1925 and taught there until 1928, when he returned to Berlin to concentrate on stage design and film.

In 1930 he participated in the Internationale Werkbund Ausstellung in Paris. The artist settled in Amsterdam in 1934, the year of a major retrospective of his work at the Stedelijk Museum there. In 1935, as a result of the growing Nazi threat, Moholy-Nagy moved to London; there he worked as a designer for various companies and on films and associated with Gabo, Barbara Hepworth, and Henry Moore. In 1937 he was appointed director of the New Bauhaus School of Industrial Arts in Chicago, which failed after less than a year because of financial problems. Moholy-Nagy established his own School of Design in Chicago in 1938 and in 1940 gave his first summer classes in rural Illinois. He joined the American Abstract Artists group in 1941 and in 1944 became a United States citizen. His book *Vision in Motion* was published in 1947, after his death on November 24, 1946, in Chicago.

62. A II. 1924

Oil on canvas, 45⅝ × 53⅝ in. (115.8 × 136.5 cm.)
Acquired 1943

By 1922 Moholy-Nagy had eliminated all references to representational subject matter. He sought to redefine painting in terms of modern technology. *A II* is related to Moholy-Nagy's coeval experiments in camera-less photography ("photograms"), painting on transparent supports, and projection of color transparencies on screens ("painting-with-light"). In *A II* the repetition of the red disc and overlapping parallelograms suggests the light projection of a design on two screens. The Constructivist idiom of this picture reflects Moholy-Nagy's knowledge of El Lissitzky's and Malevich's work.

KURT SCHWITTERS

1887–1948. Herman Edward Karl Julius Schwitters was born in Hannover on June 20, 1887. He attended the Kunstgewerbeschule in Hannover from 1908 to 1909 and from 1909 to 1914 studied at the Kunstakademie Dresden. After serving as a draftsman in the military in 1917, Schwitters experimented with Cubist and Expressionist styles. In 1918 he made his first collages and in 1919 invented the term "Merz," which he was to apply to all his creative activities: poetry as well as collage and construction. That year also marked the beginning of his friendship with Arp and Raoul Hausmann. Schwitters's earliest "Merzbilder" date from 1919, the year of his first exhibition at the gallery of Der Sturm, Berlin, and the first publication of his writings in the periodical *Der Sturm*. Schwitters showed at the Société Anonyme in New York in 1920.

In 1922 Schwitters met Van Doesburg, whose De Stijl principles influenced his work. About 1923 the artist started to make his first *Merzbau,* a fantastic structure he built over a number of years; the *Merzbau* grew to occupy much of his Hannover studio. During this period he also worked in typography. The artist contributed to the Parisian review *Cercle et Carré* in 1930; in 1932 he joined the Paris-based Abstraction-Création group and wrote for their organ of the same name. He participated in the "Cubism and Abstract Art" and "Fantastic Art, Dada, Surrealism" exhibitions of 1936 at The Museum of Modern Art, New York.

The Nazi regime banned Schwitters's work as *Entartete Kunst* (degenerate art) in 1937. That same year the artist fled to Lysaker, Norway, where he constructed a second *Merzbau*. After the German invasion of Norway in 1940, Schwitters escaped to England, where he was interned for over a year. He settled in London following his release, but moved to Little Langdale in the Lake District in 1945. There, helped by a stipend from The Museum of Modern Art, he began work on a third *Merzbau* in 1947. The project was left unfinished when Schwitters died on January 8, 1948, in Kendal, England.

63. MERZBILD 5 B (PICTURE-RED-HEART-CHURCH). April 26, 1919

(Merzbild 5 B [Bild-Rot-Herz-Kirche])
Collage, tempera, and crayon on cardboard,
32⅞ × 23¾ in. (83.5 × 60.2 cm.)
Acquired 1952

Schwitters related that he "could not see the reason why old tickets, driftwood, cloak-room tabs, wires and wheel parts, buttons and old rubbish found in the attic and in refuse dumps should not be a material for painting just as good as the colours made in factories. I called my new works that employed any such materials 'MERZ.' This is the second syllable of 'Kommerz.' It arose in the MERZ Picture, a work which showed, underneath abstract shapes, the word MERZ, cut from an advertisement of KOMMERZ UND PRIVATBANK and pasted on. This word MERZ had itself become part of the picture by adjustment to the other parts, and so it had to be there." (W. Schmalenbach, "Kurt Schwitters," *Art International,* vol. IV, Sept. 1960, p. 58.)

In *Merzbild 5 B* Schwitters cut several pieces of newspaper, pasted them down, covered them with circular and triangular painted areas, added smaller pieces of paper and a canceled postage stamp, and drew three images: a heart, a church, and the number 69. The pictorial organization is determined by the arrangement of the printed matter and by the emphatic diagonal and curvilinear elements. Through an additive method of composition involving inventively utilized found objects, Schwitters produced hundreds of these "Merzbilder."

MAX ERNST 1891–1976.

Max Ernst was born on April 2, 1891, in Brühl, Germany. He enrolled in the University at Bonn in 1909 to study philosophy but soon abandoned that pursuit to concentrate on art. At this time he was interested in psychology and the art of the mentally ill. In 1911 Ernst became friends with August Macke and joined the Rheinische Expressionisten group in Bonn. Ernst showed for the first time in 1912 at the Galerie Feldman in Cologne. At the Sonderbund exhibition of that year in Cologne he saw the work of Van Gogh, Cézanne, Munch, and Picasso. In 1913 he met Apollinaire and Robert Delaunay and traveled to Paris. Ernst participated that same year in the Erster Deutscher Herbstsalon (First German Autumn Salon). In 1914 he met Arp, who was to become a lifelong friend.

Despite military service throughout World War I, Ernst was able to continue painting and to exhibit in Berlin at the gallery of Der Sturm in 1916. He returned to Cologne in 1918. The next year he produced his first collages and founded the short-lived Cologne Dada movement with Johannes Theodor Baargeld; they were joined by Arp and others. In 1921 Ernst exhibited for the first time in Paris, at the Galerie Au Sans Pareil. He was involved in Surrealist activities in the early twenties with the poets Paul Eluard and André Breton. In 1925 Ernst executed his first frottages, or rubbings, in which the design was created by placing a piece of paper on a textured surface and rubbing over it with a pencil. A series of these frottages was published in his book *Histoire Naturelle* in 1926. He collaborated with Joan Miró on designs for Sergei Diaghilev's Ballets Russes that same year. The first of his collage-novels, *La Femme 100 têtes*, was published in 1929. The following year he collaborated with Salvador Dali and Luis Buñuel on the film *L'Age d'or*.

His first American show was held at the Julien Levy Gallery, New York, in 1932. In 1936 Ernst was represented in the "Fantastic Art, Dada, Surrealism" exhibition at The Museum of Modern Art in New York. In 1939 he was interned in France as an enemy alien. Ernst was able to flee in 1941 to the United States, where he lived until 1953. That year he resettled in France. He received the Grand Prize for Painting at the Venice Biennale in 1954. The artist was honored with numerous major retrospectives in the postwar years, the most recent of which took place at The Solomon R. Guggenheim Museum in 1975. Ernst died on April 1, 1976, in Paris.

64. AN ANXIOUS FRIEND. Summer 1944
(Un Ami empressé)
Bronze, 26⅜ in. (67 cm.) high
Fifth of nine casts made in 1957 from original plaster
of 1944 by Modern Art Foundry, Long Island
Gift, Dominique and John de Menil, 1959

During the summer of 1944, when he lived in Great River, Long Island, Ernst turned his attention to sculpture, a medium in which hc had not worked for a decade. He was influenced by the Surrealist sculpture familiar to him in Europe in the 1930s—most notably, that of his friend Alberto Giacometti. Like Giacometti's *Spoon Woman* (pl. 68), Ernst's *An Anxious Friend* exhibits the artist's knowledge of Primitive art, possesses an emphatic frontality, and is amusingly endowed with female attributes. Ernst employed found objects in making the plaster: he decorated the front with drill bits and fashioned the figure's round mouth and eyes from a set of aluminum measuring spoons.

Although he worked episodically in this medium, Ernst's sculpture is not central to his oeuvre. Consistent with his paintings and drawings, *An Anxious Friend* commands an insistent presence and provokes the imagination.

ALBERTO GIACOMETTI 1901–1966. Alberto Giacometti was born on October 10, 1901, in Borgonovo, Switzerland, and grew up in the nearby town of Stampa. His father, Giovanni, was a Post-Impressionist painter. From 1919
to 1920 he studied painting at the Ecole des Beaux-Arts and sculpture and drawing at the Ecole des Arts et Métiers
in Geneva. In 1920 he traveled to Italy, where he was impressed by the Cézannes and Archipenkos at the Venice
Biennale. He was also deeply affected by Primitive and Egyptian art and by the masterpieces of Giotto and Tin-
toretto. In 1922 Giacometti settled in Paris, making frequent visits to Stampa. From time to time over the next
several years he attended Emile-Antoine Bourdelle's sculpture classes at the Académie de la Grande Chaumière.

In 1927 the artist moved into a studio with his brother Diego, his lifelong companion and assistant, and exhibited
his sculpture for the first time at the Salon des Tuileries, Paris. His first show in Switzerland, shared with his
father, was held at the Galerie Aktuaryus in Zürich in 1927. The following year Giacometti met André Masson and
by 1930 he was a participant in the Surrealist circle. His first one-man show took place in 1932 at the Galerie Pierre

68. SPOON WOMAN. 1926
(Femme-cuiller)
Bronze, 57 in. (144.7 cm.) high
Third of six casts made in 1954 from original plaster
of 1926 by Susse Fondeur, Paris
Acquired 1955

For a short time in the mid-1920s Giacometti experimented with Cubism, soon developing a personal Cubist sculptural style. In *Spoon Woman* he assimilates the
Cubist innovations of Lipchitz and Henri Laurens. Yet

the work also reveals the influence of Primitive art and
Surrealism. There are clear similarities to Cycladic
sculpture and to certain formal characteristics of African sculpture—such as the equivalence of convexity
and concavity and the arbitrary figure proportions—
which had already been absorbed into Cubist sculpture
generally. However, the enlargement of the female torso
into an oversized, spoonlike hollow, with its inverted
reference to pregnancy, foreshadows Giacometti's brilliant explorations during the later 1920s and 1930s of
a Surrealist world arising from subconscious dreams
and emotions.

in Paris. In 1934 his first American solo exhibition opened at the Julien Levy Gallery in New York. During the early 1940s he became friends with Picasso, Jean-Paul Sartre, and Simone de Beauvoir. In 1942 Giacometti moved to Geneva, where he associated with the publisher Albert Skira.

He returned to Paris in 1946. In 1948 he was given a one-man show at the Pierre Matisse Gallery in New York. The artist's friendship with Samuel Beckett began about 1951. In 1955 he was honored with major retrospectives at the Arts Council Gallery in London and The Solomon R. Guggenheim Museum in New York. He received the Sculpture Prize at the Carnegie International in Pittsburgh in 1961 and the First Prize for Sculpture at the Venice Biennale of 1962, where he was given his own exhibition area. In 1965 Giacometti exhibitions were organized by the Tate Gallery in London, The Museum of Modern Art in New York, the Louisiana Museum in Humlebaek, Denmark, and the Stedelijk Museum in Amsterdam. That same year he was awarded the Grand National Prize for Art by the French government. Giacometti died on January 11, 1966, in Chur, Switzerland.

69. NOSE. 1947

(Le Nez)

Bronze, wire, rope, and steel, 15 × 3 × 26 in.
(38 × 7.5 × 66 cm.)

Fifth of six casts made in 1965 from plaster by Susse Fondeur, Paris

Acquired 1966

About 1947 Giacometti ceased making minute sculptures, and his tall, thin skeletal figures began to appear. In *Nose* and *Hand*, both done in 1947, the artist en-larged a detail to such a degree that it would be impossible for him to realize the whole figure. As in *Hand* and *Man Pointing* of the same year, he has elongated forms for expressive effect and in accordance with his perception of the subject. Through the introduction of a steel cage in this sculpture, Giacometti has located the head within spatial confines, although the nose protrudes beyond them. The investigation of space preoccupies the artist here as it had in the early 1940s, when he made extremely small figures on large bases, and as it would during the next years in group compositions like *City Square* and *The Cage*.

Max Beckmann 1884–1950. Max Beckmann was born in Leipzig on February 12, 1884. He began to study art with Carl Frithjof Smith at the Grossherzogliche Kunstschule in Weimar in 1900 and made his first visit to Paris in 1903–4. During this period Beckmann began his lifelong practice of keeping a diary, or *Tagebuch*. In the autumn of 1904 he settled in Berlin.

In 1913 the artist's first one-man show took place at the Galerie Cassirer in Berlin. He was discharged for reasons of health from the medical corps of the German army in 1915 and settled in Frankfurt. In 1925 Beckmann's work was included in the exhibition "Die Neue Sachlichkeit" (The New Objectivity) in Mannheim, and he was appointed professor at the Städelsches Kunstinstitut in Frankfurt. His first show in the United States took place at J. B. Neumann's New Art Circle in New York in 1926. A large retrospective of his work was held at the Kunsthalle Mannheim in 1928. From 1929 to 1932 he continued to teach in Frankfurt but spent time in Paris in the winters. It was during these years that Beckmann began to use the triptych format. When the Nazis came to power in 1933, Beckmann lost his teaching position and moved to Berlin. In 1937 his work was included in the Nazis' exhibition of *Entartete Kunst* (degenerate art). The day after the show opened in Munich in July 1937, the artist and his wife left Germany for Amsterdam, where they remained until 1947. In 1938 he was given the first of numerous exhibitions at Curt Valentin's Buchholz Gallery in New York.

Beckmann traveled to Paris and the south of France in 1947 and later that year went to the United States to teach at the School of Fine Arts at Washington University in St. Louis. The first Beckmann retrospective in the United States took place in 1948 at the City Art Museum of St. Louis. The artist taught at the University of Colorado in Boulder during the summer of 1949 and that autumn at the Brooklyn Museum School. Thus, in 1949, the Beckmanns moved to New York and the artist was awarded First Prize in the exhibition "Painting in the United States, 1949," at the Carnegie Institute in Pittsburgh. He died on December 27, 1950, in New York.

70. Paris Society. 1931
(Gesellschaft Paris)
Oil on canvas, 43 × 69⅛ in. (109.3 × 175.6 cm.)
Acquired 1970

Paris Society dates primarily from 1931 when Beckmann was in Frankfurt and in Paris during the winter. However, its conception originated as early as 1925, and the artist reworked the canvas in Amsterdam in 1947. Fifteen people are presented in a room with mirrors on the rear wall; two small background figures and the large chandelier are actually reflections of activity taking place in front of the picture plane. Not only the compressed space but also the bold, black outlines create tensions within the picture.

Although the figures are not portraits, certain individuals can be identified. In the center is Beckmann's friend Prince Rohan; a drawing for this figure dated October 30, 1931, is in the collection of Catherine Viviano, New York. The German ambassador in Paris, Leopold von Hoesch, is depicted with his hands covering his face at the right. The character as well as the title of the picture assumed its present form in 1931.

HENRY MOORE 1898–1986.

Henry Spencer Moore was born on July 30, 1898, in Castleford, Yorkshire, the son of a miner. Despite an early desire to become a sculptor, Moore began his career as a teacher in Castleford. After military service in World War I he attended Leeds School of Art on an ex-serviceman's grant. In 1921 he won a Royal Exhibition Scholarship to study sculpture at the Royal Academy of Art in London. Moore became interested in the Mexican, Egyptian, and African sculpture at the British Museum. He was appointed Instructor of Sculpture at the Royal Academy in 1924, a post he held for the next seven years. A Royal Academy traveling scholarship allowed Moore to visit Italy in 1925; there he saw the frescoes of Giotto and Masaccio and the late sculpture of Michelangelo. Moore's first one-man show of sculpture was held at the Warren Gallery, London, in 1928.

In the 1930s Moore was a member of Unit One, a group of advanced artists organized by Paul Nash, and was close friends with Ben Nicholson, Barbara Hepworth, and the critic Herbert Read. From 1932 to 1939 he taught at the Chelsea School of Art. He was an important force in the English Surrealist movement, although he was not entirely committed to its doctrines; Moore participated in the "International Surrealist Exhibition" at the New Burlington Galleries, London, in 1936. In 1940 he was appointed an official war artist and was commissioned by the War Artists Advisory Committee to execute drawings of life in underground bomb shelters. From 1940 to 1943 the artist concentrated almost entirely on drawing. His first retrospective took place at Temple Newsam, Leeds, in 1941. In 1943 he received a commission from the Church of St. Matthew, Northampton, to carve a *Madonna and Child*; this sculpture was the first in an important series of family group sculptures. Moore was given his first major retrospective abroad by The Museum of Modern Art, New York, in 1946. He won the International Prize for Sculpture at the Venice Biennale of 1948.

Moore executed several important public commissions in the 1950s, among them *Reclining Figure* (1956–58) for the UNESCO Building in Paris. In 1963 the artist was awarded the British Order of Merit. A major retrospective of his sculpture was held at the Forte di Belvedere, Florence, in 1972. Moore died on August 31, 1986, in Much Hadham, Hertfordshire.

71. UPRIGHT FIGURE. 1956–60
Elm wood, 111 in. (282 cm.) high
Acquired 1960

When The Solomon R. Guggenheim Foundation commissioned him to do a sculpture in 1956, Moore commenced carving a horizontal reclining figure which was related to his bronze *Reclining Figure* of 1956. As he worked, the artist transformed the Guggenheim's sculpture into a vertical composition. He has stated that "although, of course, I changed it considerably, it shows the great importance of gravity in sculpture. Lying down, the figure looked static, whilst upright it takes on movement, and because it is working against gravity it looks almost as though it is climbing." (J. Hedgecoe and H. Moore, *Henry Moore*, New York, 1968, p. 280.)

The towering female figure is attached to the elm block and can, therefore, be defined as a high relief. The sculpture's rough surface bears visible evidence of how Moore carved directly into the wood, a technique not often encountered in his mature work.

MATTA b. 1911. Roberto Sebastian Antonio Matta Echaurren was born on November 11, 1911, in Santiago, Chile. After studying architecture at the Universidad Católica in Santiago, Matta went to Paris in 1934 to work as an apprentice to the architect Le Corbusier. By the mid-thirties he knew the poet Federico García Lorca, Dali, and André Breton; in 1937 he left Le Corbusier's atelier and joined the Surrealist movement. That same year Matta's drawings were included in the Surrealist exhibition at Galerie Wildenstein in Paris. He began painting with oils in 1938, executing a series of fantastic landscapes, which he called "inscapes" or "psychological morphologies."

In 1939 Matta fled Europe for New York, where he associated with other Surrealist emigrés including Ernst, Yves Tanguy, André Masson, and Breton. The Julien Levy Gallery in New York presented a one-man show of his paintings in 1940, and he was included in the "Artists in Exile" exhibition at the Pierre Matisse Gallery in New York in 1942. During the forties Matta's painting anticipated many innovations of the Abstract Expressionists and significantly influenced a number of New York School artists, in particular his friends Arshile Gorky and Robert Motherwell. Toward the end of the war he evolved increasingly monstrous imagery; the appearance of mechanical forms and cinematic effects in Matta's work reflects the influence of Duchamp, whom he met in 1944. He broke with the Surrealists in 1948 and returned to Europe, settling in Rome in 1953. A mural for the UNESCO Building in Paris was executed by the artist in 1956. In 1957 he was honored with a major retrospective at The Museum of Modern Art in New York. His work was exhibited in Berlin in 1970 and Hannover in 1974. The artist now lives in Tarquinia, Italy, and Paris.

72. YEARS OF FEAR. 1941
Oil on canvas, 44 × 56 in. (111.8 × 142.2 cm.)
Acquired 1972

Like other canvases Matta painted in the early 1940s, *Years of Fear* contains changing, amorphous shapes within a landscape space that lacks either precise topography or a horizon line. He has thinly applied pigment in swirling patterns, focusing on colorful, sometimes jewel-like nuggets and structuring the canvas with weblike lines. The linear patterns establish spatial recession, link various parts of the composition, and contribute a strong stabilizing element. The artist recalls that he painted *Years of Fear* in New York at the beginning of 1941, before going to Mexico in May. After his Mexican sojourn, the yellow and gray tonalities of this picture would be replaced by more intense and brilliant colors. Although his pictorial vocabulary has evolved over the decades, Matta's plastic imagination remains consistent and his meaning continues to elude specific interpretation.

RUFINO TAMAYO

b. 1899. Rufino Tamayo was born on August 26, 1899, in Oaxaca, Mexico. Orphaned by 1911, he moved to Mexico City to live with an aunt who sent him to commercial school. Tamayo began taking drawing lessons in 1915 and by 1917 had left commercial school to devote himself entirely to the study of art. In 1921 he was appointed head of the department of ethnographic drawing at the Museo Nacional de Arqueología, Mexico City, where his duties included drawing pre-Columbian objects in the museum's collection. Tamayo integrated the forms and slaty tones of pre-Columbian ceramics into his early still lifes and portraits of the men and women of Mexico.

The first exhibition of his work in the United States was held at the Weyhe Gallery, New York, in 1926. He received the first of many mural commissions from the Escuela Nacional de Música in Mexico City in 1932. In 1936 the artist moved to New York, and throughout the late thirties and early forties the Valentine Gallery, New York, gave him shows. He taught for nine years, beginning in 1938, at the Dalton School in New York. In 1948 the artist's first retrospective took place at the Instituto de Bellas Artes, Mexico City. Tamayo was influenced by European modernism during his stay in New York and later when he traveled in Europe and settled in Paris in 1957. He executed a mural for the UNESCO Building in Paris in 1958. Tamayo returned to Mexico City in 1964, making it his permanent home. The French government named him Chevalier and Officier de la Légion d'Honneur in 1956 and 1969 respectively, and he has been the recipient of numerous other honors and awards. His work has been exhibited internationally in group and one-man shows, one of the most important of which was a retrospective at the 1977 São Paulo Bienal. In 1979 Tamayo was honored with a retrospective at The Solomon R. Guggenheim Museum. The artist lives and works in Mexico City.

73. WOMAN IN GREY. 1959
(Mujer en gris)
Oil on canvas, 76¾ × 51 in. (195 × 129.5 cm.)
Acquired 1959

Tamayo's orientation toward School of Paris artists does not obscure the inspiration he derives from his Mexican heritage. *Woman in Grey* combines austerity and a warm earthiness of palette with a female figure reminiscent of Picasso's work of the late 1920s and early 1930s. The stylized contour of the woman's body is repeated in the decorative background pattern, and a consistently painted surface unifies the canvas. Tamayo's commitment to figure painting is demonstrated in a related contemporary painting, *Woman in White* of 1959 (Collection Milwaukee Art Center), and in later canvases such as *Dancer* of 1977 (Collection The Solomon R. Guggenheim Museum).

JEAN DUBUFFET 1901–1985. Jean Dubuffet was born in Le Havre on July 31, 1901. He attended art classes in his youth and in 1918 moved to Paris to study at the Académie Julian, which he left after six dissatisfying months. During this time Dubuffet met Suzanne Valadon, Raoul Dufy, Léger, and Max Jacob and became fascinated with Hans Prinzhorn's book on psychopathic art; he was also interested in literature, music, philosophy, and linguistics. In 1923 and 1924 he traveled to Italy and South America respectively. Upon his return he gave up painting for about ten years, supporting himself first as an industrial draftsman and then by working in the family wine business. After much vacillation between careers in art and business, he committed himself entirely to becoming an artist in 1942.

Dubuffet's first one-man exhibition was held at the Galerie René Drouin in Paris in 1944. During the forties the artist associated with Charles Ratton, Jean Paulhan, Georges Limbour, and André Breton. His style and subject matter in this period owed a debt to Klee and Alfred Jarry. Starting in 1945 Dubuffet collected what he called *Art Brut*—spontaneous, direct works by individuals, often mental patients, not influenced by professional artists. The Pierre Matisse Gallery gave him his first one-man show in New York in 1947.

74. WILL TO POWER. January 1946
(Volonté de puissance)
Oil, pebbles, sand, and glass on canvas, 45¾ × 35 in. (116.2 × 88.9 cm.)
Acquired 1964

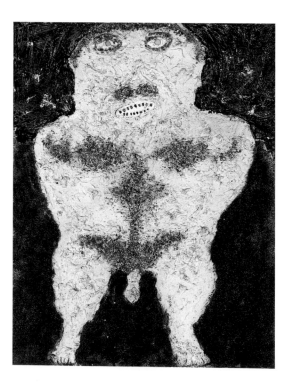

In *Will to Power* the frontal male nude fills the canvas from top edge to bottom, overwhelming the pictorial space. This *"personnage incivil,"* as Dubuffet called the figure, is seen against "a sky of trivial and violent blue." (*Mirobolus, Macadam & Cie: Hautes Pâtes de J. Dubuffet*, exh. cat., Paris, 1946, p. 56.) The stocky, muscular man with his arms behind his back presents an image of masculine brutality. Dubuffet used a variety of materials to create the coarse, gritty, heavily impastoed surface and employed stones for the man's teeth and shiny inlaid glass fragments for his eyes.

Dubuffet's title, *Will to Power*, refers to a central concept in the philosophy of Friedrich Nietzsche. The concept was popularized after Nietzsche's death and in this attenuated form was incorporated into the ideology of Nazism. Thus, Dubuffet's image appears to be a caricature of the "will to power" interpreted as romanticized masculine aggression.

From 1951 to 1952 Dubuffet lived in New York; he then returned to Paris, where a retrospective of his work took place at the Cercle Volney in 1954. His first museum retrospective occurred in 1957 at the Schloss Morsbroich, Leverkusen, Germany. Major Dubuffet exhibitions have since been held at the Musée des Arts Décoratifs, Paris; The Museum of Modern Art, New York; The Art Institute of Chicago; the Stedelijk Museum, Amsterdam; the Tate Gallery, London; and The Solomon R. Guggenheim Museum in New York. In 1962 he began a series of paintings known as L'Hourloupe; these were exhibited at the Palazzo Grassi in Venice in 1964. A collection of Dubuffet's writings, *Prospectus et tous écrits suivants*, was published in 1967, the same year he started his architectural structures. Soon thereafter he began numerous commissions for monumental outdoor sculptures, some of which were shown at The Art Institute of Chicago in 1969. In 1971 he produced his first theater props, the "*practicables.*" The following year his *Group of Four Trees* was erected at Chase Manhattan Plaza, New York, and he gave his collection of *Art Brut* to the city of Lausanne. Dubuffet died on May 12, 1985, in Paris.

75. *NUNC STANS. May 16–June 5, 1965*
Vinyl on canvas, three panels, each 63¾ × 107⅞ in.
(161.9 × 274 cm.)
Acquired 1974

Dubuffet created *Nunc Stans* in May-June 1965 as part of a commission for wall decorations to go in the entrance hall of the new Faculté des Lettres at Nanterre, France. Although the project was later abandoned, many studies exist for *Nunc Stans*. Dubuffet used primary colors and black and white vinyl paint in the large-scale panels belonging to the Guggenheim. The smooth surface, the bold, decorative quality, and the pattern of interlocking pictographs are typical of the Hourloupe cycle. Dubuffet invented the name "L'Hourloupe" to refer to the series he began in July 1962. In this cycle traditional figure-ground relationship is destroyed; instead, there is a play of image against image.

FRANCIS BACON b. 1909.

Francis Bacon was born in Dublin on October 28, 1909. At the age of sixteen he moved to London and subsequently lived for about two years in Berlin and Paris. Bacon never attended art school but began to draw and work in watercolor about 1926–27. Picasso's work had a decisive influence on his painting until the mid-1940s. Upon his return to London in 1929 he established himself as a furniture designer and interior designer. He began to use oils in the autumn of that year. His work was included in group exhibitions in London at the Mayor Gallery in 1933 and at Thos. Agnew and Sons in 1937.

Bacon's mature style emerged about 1944, and his first one-man show took place at the Hanover Gallery in London in 1949. From the mid-1940s to the early 1950s Bacon's work reflects the influence of Surrealism and reveals the artist's predilection for placing his figures in interior spaces. He avoids the static image of traditional figure painting and attempts to show his subjects in motion, frequently using the technique of blurring to suggest mobility. He has dwelt upon such images as a person screaming and an open mouth. In the 1950s Bacon drew on sources as varied as Diego Velázquez, Van Gogh, and Eadweard Muybridge. Receptive to photographic images in the conception of his paintings, Bacon clips illustrations from newspapers and magazines. Since the mid-1960s his canvases reveal a greater sense of depth, brighter and more varied colors, and the use of foreshortened and twisting forms to create a nightmare vision. Major retrospectives of Bacon's work opened at The Solomon R. Guggenheim Museum in 1963 and at the Grand Palais in Paris in 1971; paintings from 1968 to 1974 were exhibited at The Metropolitan Museum of Art, New York, in 1975. The artist lives in London.

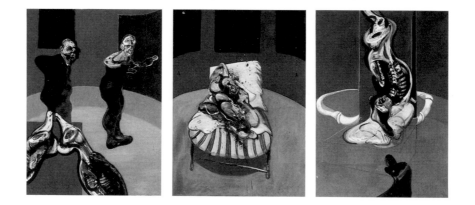

76. THREE STUDIES FOR A CRUCIFIXION
March 1962
Oil with sand on canvas, three panels, each 78 × 57 in. (198.2 × 144.8 cm.)
Acquired 1966

Bacon first grouped three panels together in 1944 in the major work *Three Studies for Figures at the Base of a Crucifixion* (Collection Tate Gallery, London). Eighteen years later he returned to the triptych format with the Guggenheim's *Three Studies for a Crucifixion*. While the artist was undoubtedly responding to representations of the Crucifixion by Grünewald, Picasso, and by his friend Roy de Maistre, he does not believe in its Christian meaning. For Bacon it is not a religious subject but the ultimate example of man's inhumanity to man.

The artist worked on the three panels separately during a two-week period in March 1962 when he was drinking heavily. As he completed them, they evolved into a triptych and were finished together; parts of the left panel were reworked later the same month. Bacon finds that many images come to him at once, and that the triptych format allows for the expression of such simultaneity without implying any narrative sequence. As the artist has explained, the undulating figure in the right panel was inspired by the Christ figure in Cimabue's Crucifixion, which always reminded him of a worm crawling down the cross. The significance of the two figures in the left panel remains mysterious, while the foreground images of meat and the slaughterhouse are associated with the physical aspects of the Crucifixion. The violence in the center panel has decidedly modern connotations made explicit by the victim's smashed head, the bullet holes, and the bloodstained bed and intensified by the expressive reds, oranges, and blacks of the three panels.

ASGER JORN

1914–1973. Asger Jorn was born Asger Oluf Jørgensen at Vejrum in Jutland, Denmark, on March 3, 1914. In the autumn of 1936 he visited Paris, where he studied at Léger's Académie Contemporaine. During the war Jorn remained in Denmark, painting canvases that reflect the influence of Ensor, Kandinsky, Klee, and Miró and contributing to the magazine *Helhesten*.

Jorn traveled to Swedish Lapland in the summer of 1946, met George Constant in Paris that autumn, and spent six months in Djerba, Tunisia, in 1947–48. His first one-man exhibition in Paris took place in 1948 at the Galerie Breteau. At about the same time the COBRA (an acronym for Copenhagen, Brussels, Amsterdam) movement was founded by Karel Appel, Constant, Corneille, Christian Dotremont, Jorn, and Joseph Noiret. The group's unifying doctrine was complete freedom of expression, especially as regarded color and brushwork. Jorn edited monographs of the Bibliothèque Cobra before disassociating himself from the movement.

In 1951 he returned, poor and ill, to Silkeborg, his hometown in Denmark. He began his intensive work in ceramics in 1953. The following year he settled in Albisola, Italy, and participated in a continuation of COBRA called Mouvement International pour un Bauhaus Imaginiste. Jorn's activities included painting, collage, book illustration, prints, drawings, ceramics, tapestries, murals, and, in his last years, sculpture. He participated in the Situationist International movement from 1957 to 1961 and worked on a study of early Scandinavian art between 1961 and 1965. After the mid-1950s Jorn divided his time between Paris and Albisola. His first one-man show in New York took place in 1962 at the Lefebre Gallery. From 1966 onward Jorn concentrated on oil painting and traveled frequently, visiting Cuba, England and Scotland, the United States, and the Orient. He died on May 1, 1973, in Aarhus, Denmark.

77. GREEN BALLET. 1960
(Il balletto verde)
Oil on canvas, 57⅛ × 78⅞ in. (145 × 200 cm.)
Acquired 1962

Jorn's paintings are generally less figurative in inspiration than those of his COBRA colleagues. In this canvas, where bright colors are applied in a seeming frenzy, control is established by the large sweeping movements and the asymmetrically balanced color shapes. The artist's title suggests the floating, turning shapes and the figures splayed out across the canvas. The palette of predominant greens with red, yellow, and blue is frequently encountered in Jorn's work, as is the expressive function of the heavily applied pigment. A sense of genesis, produced by the balance between creative and destructive forces, emerges as the artist's primary concern.

JEAN IPOUSTÉGUY b. 1920. Jean-Robert Ipoustéguy was born on January 6, 1920, in Dun-sur-Meuse, France. In 1938 he moved to Paris and studied in the atelier of the artist Robert Lesbounit. Ipoustéguy primarily painted and designed tapestries and stained-glass windows in the 1940s. In 1949 he moved to Choisy-le-Roi, near Paris, and from that time devoted himself exclusively to sculpture, working mostly in bronze until 1967. His sculpture was first exhibited in 1956 at the Salon de Mai, Paris. In 1962 the Galerie Claude Bernard, Paris, gave Ipoustéguy his first one-man show. In 1964 he was awarded a prize from the Bright Foundation at the Venice Biennale; his first one-man exhibition in the United States took place at the Albert Loeb Gallery in New York.

In the summer of 1967 Ipoustéguy began to work primarily in Carrara marble, a medium he continues to favor today. In 1968 the city of Darmstadt awarded him its art prize, and the Galerie Claude Bernard gave him another one-man exhibition. An Ipoustéguy retrospective was mounted by the Kunsthalle in Darmstadt in 1969. The Kunsthalle Basel presented a one-man exhibition of his work in 1970, as did the Artel Galerie, Geneva, in 1974. In 1973–74 he lived in Berlin as a guest of the Deutsche Akademische Austauschdienst (German Academic Exchange Service). Ipoustéguy was given an important one-man show at the Nationalgalerie Berlin in 1974. The artist continues to exhibit at the Galerie Claude Bernard in Paris, and he lives and works in Choisy-le-Roi.

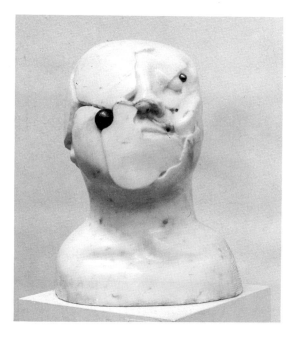

78. LENIN. 1967
(Lénine)
Marble and metal, 23 in. (58.4 cm.) high
Acquired 1968

In a work like *Lenin* Ipoustéguy exhibits his probing concern with famous historical figures as well as a characteristic tendency to refer to the art of the past: specifically to Renaissance and Mannerist sculpture. The face emerging from the stone recalls Michelangelo's figures being freed from blocks of marble. Ipoustéguy has a predilection for working in marble and for representing the human body. He achieves a strange effect of flesh and bone that proceeds from Surrealist imagery. Through the erosion of facial features and the use of ball bearings for misplaced and unmatched eyes, Ipoustéguy shatters reality.

RICHARD HAMILTON b. 1922. Richard Hamilton was born on February 24, 1922, in London. His schooling took place entirely in that city. While working in advertising in 1936, he attended classes at Westminster Technical College and St. Martin's School of Art. From 1938 to 1940 and again in 1946 Hamilton studied painting at the Royal Academy Schools. In 1948 he entered the Slade School of Fine Art. He devised and designed the 1951 exhibition "Growth and Form" at the Institute of Contemporary Art (I.C.A.) in London. In 1952 Hamilton began teaching at the Central School of Arts and Crafts in London and joined the Independent Group at I.C.A., which included Lawrence Alloway, John McHale, Eduardo Paolozzi, and others. From 1953 to 1966 he taught at King's College, University of Durham, which was to become the University of Newcastle-upon-Tyne. The show "Man, Machine, and Motion" was organized by Hamilton and presented at the Hatton Gallery, Newcastle-upon-Tyne, and at I.C.A. in 1955. He collaborated with McHale and John Voelcker on an environment for the "This is Tomorrow" exhibition of 1956 at the Whitechapel Art Gallery in London.

In 1960 Hamilton produced a typographic reproduction of Duchamp's *Green Box*. His 1963 visit to the United States familiarized him with the work of the American Pop artists. He continued his homage to Duchamp, reconstructing *The Large Glass* in 1965–66 and organizing the show "The Almost Complete Works of Marcel Duchamp" at the Tate Gallery in London the following year. In 1967 Hamilton's graphics were exhibited at the Galerie Ricke in Kassel and his paintings at the Alexandre Iolas Gallery in New York. One-man exhibitions of his work were presented by the National Gallery of Canada, Ottawa, in 1970, the Stedelijk Museum in Amsterdam in 1971, and The Solomon R. Guggenheim Museum in 1973. Hamilton lives near London.

79. *THE SOLOMON R. GUGGENHEIM (BLACK); (BLACK and WHITE); (SPECTRUM)*
1965–66
Fiberglas and cellulose, three reliefs, each 48 × 48 × 7½ in. (122 × 122 × 19 cm.)
Acquired 1967

These three reliefs belong to a series of six Hamilton made in Fiberglas from the same mold in 1965–66. A color postcard of Frank Lloyd Wright's Guggenheim Museum was the catalyst which led the artist to study photographs as well as the architect's plans for the building and then to make his own elevations, sections, and numerous preparatory sketches and prints. Each relief has the same single, large spiral form seen in false perspective, but because of the varying color schemes, each has a different appearance. The *Black and White* version accentuates the projecting spiral bands and contrasting recessions. In the *Black* relief the museum merges with reflections of the surrounding environment: its slick, glossy finish dissolving any three-dimensionality of form. In the last example the colors move through the spectrum, from red to yellow and blue to violet, vertically superimposed on the curved horizontals. Hamilton said, "Instead of *being* the rainbow, the Guggenheim is seen at the bottom of the rainbow." (J. Russell, "Richard Hamilton," *Art in America,* vol. 58, Mar. 1970, p. 118.) His other reliefs in the series are in gold, metalflake, and Neapolitan ice cream colors.

ALEXANDER CALDER

1898–1976. Alexander Calder was born on July 22, 1898, in Lawnton, Pennsylvania, into a family of artists. In 1919 he received an engineering degree from Stevens Institute of Technology in Hoboken, New Jersey. Calder attended the Art Students League in New York from 1923 to 1926, studying with Thomas Hart Benton and John Sloan among others. As a free-lance artist for the *National Police Gazette* in 1925 he spent two weeks covering the circus; his fascination with the subject dates from this time.

Calder's earliest sculptures were wire and wood animals and figures made in 1926. His first exhibition of paintings took place in 1926 at The Artist's Gallery in New York. Later that year Calder went to Paris and attended the Académie de la Grande Chaumière. In Paris he met Stanley William Hayter, exhibited at the 1926 Salon des Indépendants, and in 1927 began giving performances of his miniature circus. The first show of his wire animals and caricature portraits was held at the Weyhe Gallery, New York, in 1928. That same year he met Miró, who became his lifelong friend. Subsequently, Calder divided his time between France and the United States. In 1929 the Galerie Billiet gave him his first one-man show in Paris. He met Léger, Frederick Kiesler, and Van Doesburg and visited Mondrian's studio in 1930. Calder began to experiment with abstract sculpture at this time and in 1931–32 introduced moving parts into his work. These moving sculptures were called mobiles; the stationary constructions were to be named stabiles. He exhibited with the Abstraction-Création group in Paris in 1933. In 1943 The Museum of Modern Art in New York gave him a major one-man exhibition.

Calder won First Prize for Sculpture at the 1952 Venice Biennale. Late in the decade the artist worked extensively with gouache; from this period he executed numerous major public commissions. In 1964–65 the Guggenheim Museum presented an important Calder retrospective. He died in New York on November 11, 1976.

80. RED LILY PADS. 1956

(*Nénuphars rouges*)
Painted sheet metal, metal rods, and wire, 42 × 201 × 109 in. (106.7 × 510.6 × 276.9 cm.)
Acquired 1965

Red Lily Pads is at once an abstract composition of red-painted discs, rods, and wires, and a giant emblem of leaves floating on water. With the complex distribution of weight, Calder maintains a continually changing equilibrium. The large scale of this mobile activates the Guggenheim's interior space, and the suspension of abstract shapes exemplifies mobility and freedom.

In the 1940s Jean-Paul Sartre wrote about Calder's work: "A mobile does not suggest anything: it captures genuine living movements and shapes them. Mobiles have no meaning, make you think of nothing but themselves. They are, that is all; they are absolutes. There is more of the unpredictable about them than in any other human creation. . . . In short, although mobiles do not seek to imitate anything . . . they are nevertheless at once lyrical inventions, technical combinations of an almost mathematical quality and sensitive symbols of Nature." (J. Lipman, *Calder's Universe,* New York, 1976, p. 261.)

JOSEF ALBERS 1888–1976. Josef Albers was born on March 19, 1888, in Bottrop, Germany. From 1905 to 1908 he studied to become a teacher in Büren and then taught in Westphalian primary schools from 1908 to 1913. After attending the Königliche Kunstschule in Berlin from 1913 to 1915, he was certified as an art teacher. Albers studied art in Essen and Munich before entering the Bauhaus in Weimar in 1920. There he initially concentrated on glass painting and in 1929, as a *Bauhausgeselle* (journeyman), he reorganized the glass workshop. In 1923 he began to teach the *Vorkurs,* a basic design course. When the Bauhaus moved to Dessau in 1925, he became a *Bauhausmeister* (professor). In addition to working in glass and metal, he designed furniture and typography.

After the Bauhaus was forced to close in 1933, Albers emigrated to the United States. That same year he became head of the art department at the newly established, experimental Black Mountain College in Black Mountain, North Carolina. Albers continued to teach at Black Mountain until 1949. In 1935 he took the first of many trips to Mexico, and in 1936 was given his first one-man show in New York at J. B. Neumann's New Art Circle. He became a United States citizen in 1939. In 1949 Albers began his Homage to the Square series.

He lectured and taught at various colleges and universities throughout the United States and from 1950 to 1958 served as head of the design department at Yale University. In addition to painting, printmaking, and executing murals and architectural commissions, Albers published poetry, articles, and books on art. Thus, as a theoretician and teacher, he was an important influence on generations of young artists. A major Albers exhibition, organized by The Museum of Modern Art, New York, traveled throughout South America, Mexico, and the United States from 1965 to 1967, and a retrospective of his work was held at The Metropolitan Museum of Art, New York, in 1971. Albers lived and worked in New Haven until his death there on March 25, 1976.

81. HOMAGE TO THE SQUARE: APPARITION
1959
Oil on Masonite, 48 × 48 in. (121.9 × 121.9 cm.)
Acquired 1961

In 1949 Albers began a series of paintings exploring the possibilities of color interactions within the format of single-centered squares. *Homage to the Square: Apparition* dates from 1959 and exemplifies an arrangement of four nested squares: one of four formats evolved by the artist. While Malevich, Mondrian, and De Stijl painters had also employed the square format, Albers chose this simplest of geometric shapes and subdivided it into three or four concentric squares. Depending upon the hues juxtaposed, the colors can be seen as advancing or receding.

With a palette knife he applied unmixed oil colors to a well-primed white ground on Masonite panel. He painted each precisely measured square up to its very edge, where the next one began. Albers avoided complementary colors and, after early Homages, shunned strong color contrasts, favoring yellows and grays instead. The sharpness of contour separating squares is dependent upon the degree of contrast between adjacent hues. In *Apparition* the subdued hues of green, blue, and gray permit the central yellow square to come forward like sunlight shining through a window. Albers's lifelong preoccupation with the interaction of color and light culminated in the infinite variations of Homage to the Square.

HANS HOFMANN

1880–1966. Hans Hofmann was born on March 21, 1880, in Weissenburg, Bavaria. He was raised in Munich, where in 1898 he began to study at various art schools. The patronage of Philip Freudenberg, a Berlin art collector, enabled Hofmann to live in Paris from 1904 to 1914. In Paris he attended the Académie de la Grande Chaumière, where Matisse was also a student; he met Picasso, Braque, and other Cubists and was a friend of Robert Delaunay, who stimulated his interest in color. In 1909 Hofmann exhibited with the Secession in Berlin, and in 1910 was given his first one-man show at Paul Cassirer's gallery there. During this period he painted in a Cubist style.

At the outbreak of World War I Hofmann was in Munich; he remained there and in 1915 opened an art school, which became highly successful. The artist taught at the University of California at Berkeley during the summer of 1930. He returned to teach in California in 1931, and his first exhibition in the United States took place that summer at the California Palace of the Legion of Honor, San Francisco. In 1932 he closed his Munich school and decided to settle in the United States. His first school in New York opened in 1933 and was succeeded in 1934 by the Hans Hofmann School of Fine Arts; in 1935 he established a summer school in Provincetown, Massachusetts.

After an extended period devoted to drawing, Hofmann returned to painting in 1935, combining Cubist structure, vivid color, and emphatic gesture. He became a United States citizen in 1941. The artist's completely abstract works date from the 1940s. His first one-man show in New York took place at Peggy Guggenheim's gallery, Art of This Century, in 1944. Hofmann was an important influence upon younger artists. In 1958 he closed his schools to devote himself full time to painting. Among Hofmann's major museum exhibitions was a retrospective at The Museum of Fine Arts, Houston, 1976–77. Hans Hofmann died in New York on February 17, 1966.

82. THE GATE. 1959–60

Oil on canvas, 75⅛ × 48½ in. (190.7 × 123.2 cm.)
Acquired 1962

It is most likely that Hofmann painted *The Gate* in 1959, the year inscribed on the reverse of the canvas. Related in style to works such as *Equipoise* (1958) and *Elysium* (1960), the title suggests a stable, architectural image as do the titles *Cathedral* (1959), *City Horizon* (1959), and *The Golden Wall* (1961). Hofmann retained the easel painting format and often worked with rectangular areas of color that lined up precisely with the edges of the canvas and thus reinforced its rectangular shape.

The Gate is distinguished by vivid, radiant colors and a sense of the weight and density of paint. Against a background of freely brushed green pigment (a hue Hofmann favored), the artist has laid on oblong slabs of fully saturated color. The central red rectangle and the large yellow one above it come forward from the picture plane. Such floating rectangles, which began to appear in Hofmann's paintings about 1954–55, allow him to create complex spatial relationships between colors and shapes. The rectangular planes of color are placed on the canvas so as to produce a rhythm and tension between force and counterforce equivalent to that found in nature.

RICHARD LINDNER 1901–1978.

Richard Lindner was born in Hamburg on November 11, 1901. His childhood was spent in Nürnberg, where he studied music. He later studied art at the Akademie der bildenden Künste in Munich. During this early period he was interested in Dada and the published works of Duchamp and Picabia. Lindner spent a year in Berlin in 1928 and then returned to Munich to become art director of the publishing firm Knorr und Hirth.

In 1933, the day after the Nazis came to power, Lindner fled Germany. He settled in Paris, where he was able to work from time to time as a graphic artist. In 1939 he was interned by the French for five months; after a turbulent period, during which he served briefly in the French army and fled to Free France, he managed to escape to the United States in 1941. Living in New York, he became well known as an illustrator for *Vogue, Harper's Bazaar,* and *Fortune.* He received his United States citizenship in 1948. In 1952 Lindner abandoned illustration and began to teach painting and drawing at Pratt Institute, Brooklyn. Saul Steinberg and Hedda Sterne were among his friends.

Lindner's first one-man exhibition was held in 1954 at the Betty Parsons Gallery, New York, where his work was shown until the latter part of the decade. In 1965 he resigned from Pratt and devoted himself full time to painting. He was elected to the National Institute of Arts and Letters in 1972. A Lindner retrospective traveled to the Städtische Kunsthalle Düsseldorf and to the Musée National d'Art Moderne, Paris, in 1974. In 1977 the artist was given an important one-man show at the Museum of Contemporary Art in Chicago. On April 16, 1978, Lindner died at his home in New York.

83. THE SECRET. 1960
Oil on canvas, 50 × 40 in. (127 × 101.6 cm.)
Gift, Joachim Jean Aberbach, 1977

Lindner differentiates one portion of the canvas from another by means of flat, smoothly finished color areas. The figure of a boy seen in profile occupies the lower right; his hand holds a string which leads to the girl. Confined to a hooplike circle, she bears a strong resemblance to a china doll. The color wheel on the surface is also like a toy friction metal sparkler that Lindner owned—and is similar to the distinctive object in his painting *The Target* from the previous year (Collection Mr. and Mrs. Joseph R. Shapiro, Oak Park, Illinois). The detached spectator at the upper right attracts our attention and reminds us of the theatricality of the figure arrangement contrived by the artist. Through the compartmentalization of pictorial space and the isolation of the figures, Lindner emphasizes the secret lives of people.

A reproduction of the Guggenheim's painting appeared with the following statement by the artist:

I can not talk about painting. I have now even doubts that there is such a thing as art in general. More and more I believe in the secret behaviour of human beings. Maybe all of us are creative if we listen to the secret of our inner voice. (*Americans 1963*, exh. cat., New York, 1963, p. 60.)

JOSEPH CORNELL

1903–1972. Joseph Cornell was born on December 24, 1903, in Nyack, New York. From 1917 to 1921 he attended Phillips Academy in Andover, Massachusetts. He was an ardent collector of memorabilia and, while working as a woolen-goods salesman in New York for the next ten years, he developed a passion for ballet, literature, and the opera.

In the early thirties Cornell met Surrealist writers and artists at the Julien Levy Gallery in New York and saw Ernst's collage-novel *La Femme 100 têtes*. Cornell's early constructions of found objects were first shown in the exhibition "Surrealism," presented at the Wadsworth Atheneum in Hartford and subsequently at Julien Levy's gallery in 1932. From 1934 to 1940 Cornell supported himself by working at the Traphagen studio in New York. During these years he became familiar with Duchamp's "readymades" and Schwitters's box constructions. Cornell was included in the 1936 exhibition "Fantastic Art, Dada, Surrealism" at The Museum of Modern Art, New York. Always interested in film and cinematic techniques, he made a number of movies, including *Rose Hobart* of 1931, and wrote two film scenarios. One of these, *Monsieur Phot* of 1933, was published in 1936 in Levy's book *Surrealism*.

Cornell's first one-man exhibition took place at the Julien Levy Gallery in 1939: included was an array of objects, a number of them in shadow boxes. During the forties and fifties he made Medici boxes, boxes devoted to stage and screen personalities, Aviary constructions, Observatories, Night Skies, Winter Night Skies, and Hotel boxes. In the early 1960s Cornell stopped making new boxes and began to reconstruct old ones and to work intensively in collage. Major Cornell retrospectives were held in 1967 at the Pasadena Art Museum and The Solomon R. Guggenheim Museum, New York. In 1971 The Metropolitan Museum of Art in New York mounted an exhibition of his collages. Cornell died on December 29, 1972, at his home in Flushing, New York.

84. SPACE OBJECT BOX: "LITTLE BEAR, ETC." MOTIF. Mid 1950s–Early 1960s
Construction and collage, 11 × 17½ × 5¼ in. (28 × 44.5 × 13.3 cm.)
Acquired 1968

Within the confines of this small box Cornell has assembled two metal rods with a ring, a cork ball, a toy block, pieces of driftwood, and a map fragment of Ursa Minor (Little Bear). The representation of the Northern Sky with Little Dipper in *Space Object Box* came from a book on astronomy that belonged to the artist. Always fascinated with astronomy, he often referred to constellations and stars in his work. Cornell has extended the coordinate lines of this star map across the back wall of the box, thus incorporating the ball and ring into the celestial system. The ball positioned on the rods implies the movement of the sun across the sky, and the ring suggests the orbits of planets around the sun.

Cornell's artistic production is composed of constructions, collages, and films rather than paintings or sculptures. He combined objects and fragments he found and collected. Seen through the glass of *Space Object Box,* they are transformed into a world of their own. By isolating and juxtaposing disparate objects, Cornell formulated new relationships of space and time.

COLORPLATES

Archipenko • Lipchitz • Larionov • Malevich • Popova • Mondrian • Van Doesburg • Gabo • Pevsner •
Moholy-Nagy • Schwitters • Ernst • Arp • Miró • Giacometti • Beckmann • Moore • Matta • Tamayo •
Dubuffet • Bacon • Jorn • Ipoustéguy • Hamilton • Calder • Albers • Hofmann • Lindner • Cornell

51. ALEXANDER ARCHIPENKO
Médrano II. 1913

52. JACQUES LIPCHITZ
Standing Personage. 1916

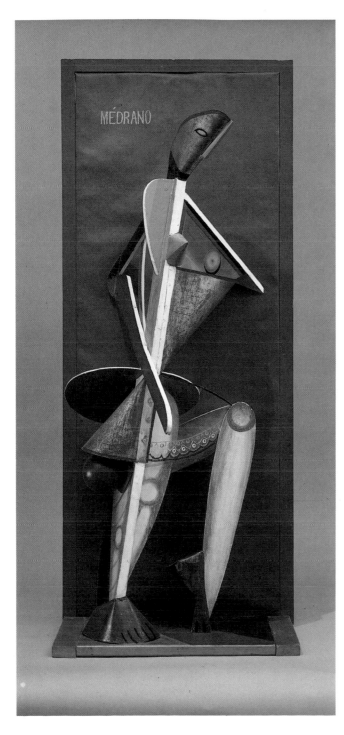

53. MIKHAIL LARIONOV *Glass.* 1912

58. PIET MONDRIAN *Composition I A.* 1930

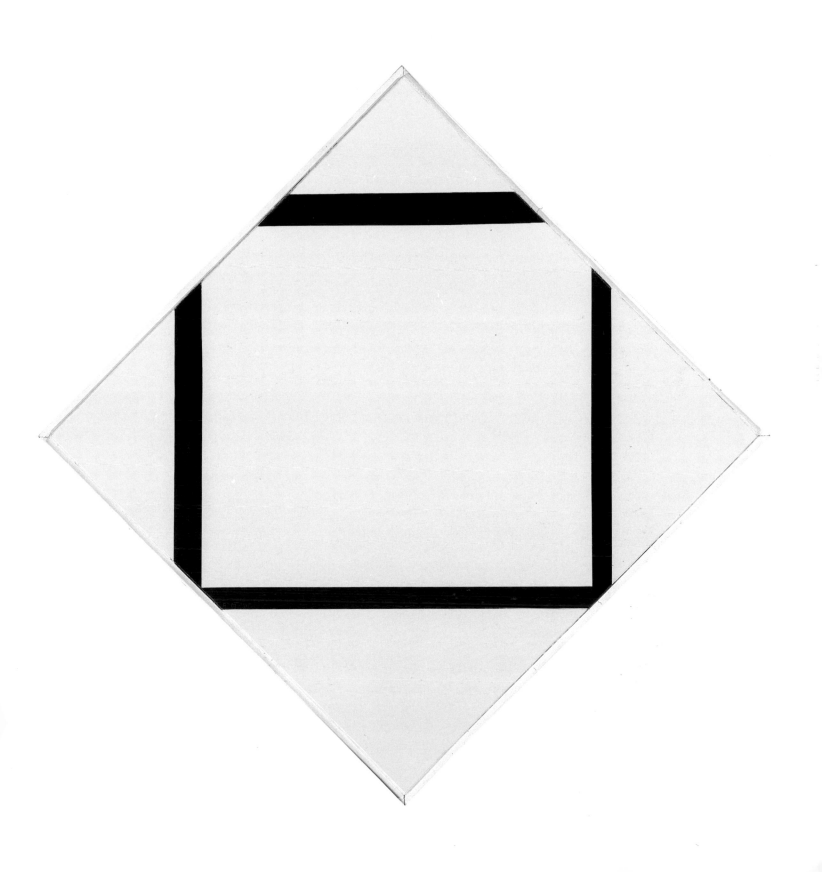

59. THEO VAN DOESBURG *Composition XI.* 1918

60. Naum Gabo
Column. c. 1923. Reconstructed in 1937

61. Antoine Pevsner
Twinned Column. 1947

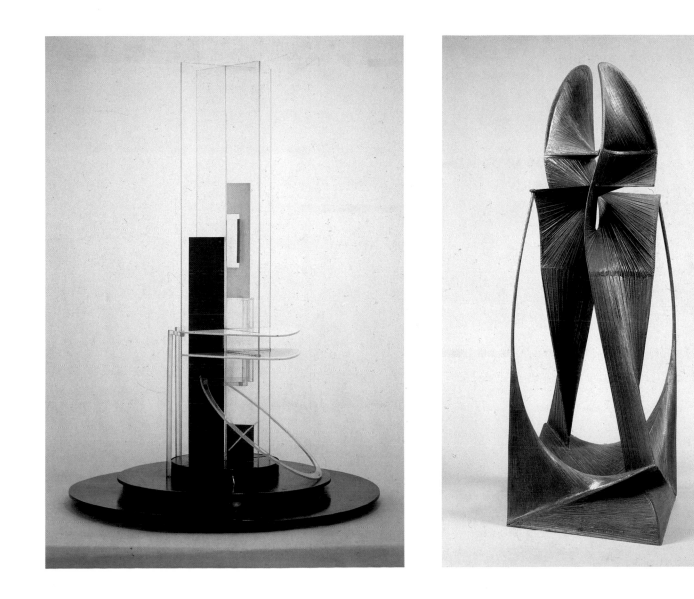

62. LÁSZLÓ MOHOLY-NAGY *A II.* 1924

64. MAX ERNST *An Anxious Friend.* 1944

65. JEAN ARP *Constellation with Five White Forms and Two Black, Variation III.* 1932

67. Joan Miró (with Josep Llorens Artigas) *Alicia.* 1965–67

68. ALBERTO GIACOMETTI *Spoon Woman.* 1926

70. MAX BECKMANN *Paris Society.* 1931

71. HENRY MOORE *Upright Figure.* 1956–60

72. MATTA *Years of Fear.* 1941

73. RUFINO TAMAYO *Woman in Grey.* 1959

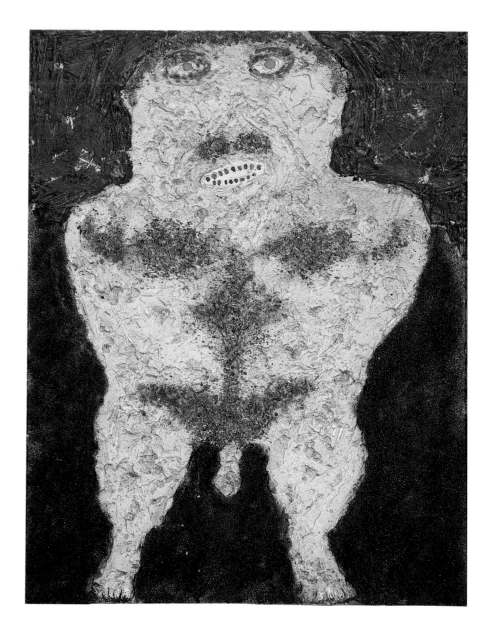

74. JEAN DUBUFFET *Will to Power.* 1946

75. JEAN DUBUFFET *Nunc Stans.* 1965

76. FRANCIS BACON *Three Studies for a Crucifixion.* 1962

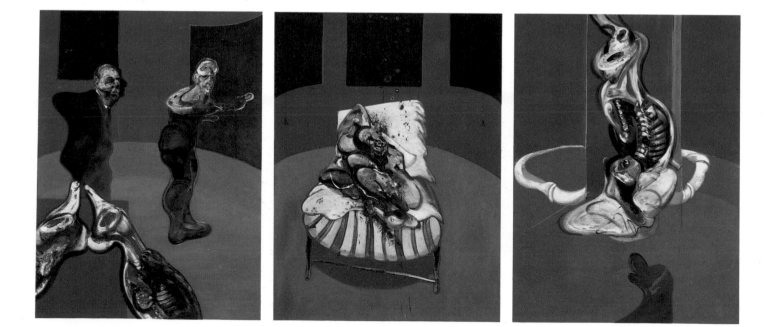

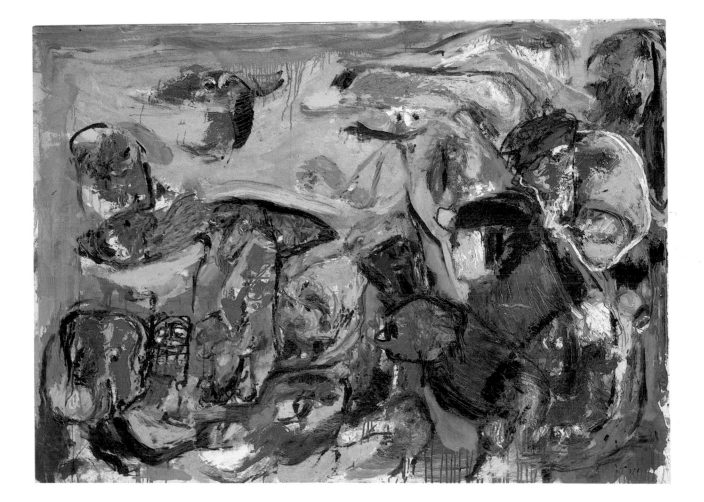

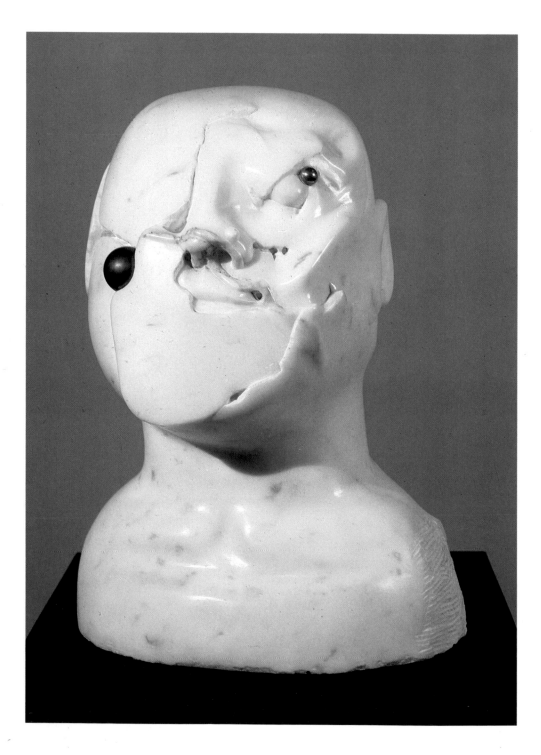

79. RICHARD HAMILTON *The Solomon R. Guggenheim (Black); (Black and White); (Spectrum).* 1965–66

80. ALEXANDER CALDER *Red Lily Pads.* 1956

81. JOSEF ALBERS *Homage to the Square: Apparition.* 1959

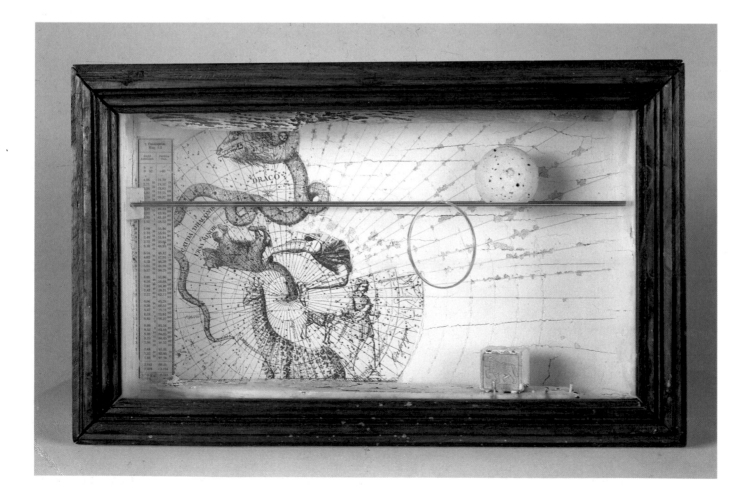

COMMENTARIES

Gorky • De Kooning • Pollock • Rothko • Gottlieb • Kline • Diebenkorn • Noguchi • Nevelson • Smith • Rauschenberg • Warhol • Lichtenstein • Louis • Kelly • Estes

ARSHILE GORKY

1904–1948. Arshile Gorky was born Vosdanik Adoian in the village of Khorkom, province of Van, Armenia, on April 15, 1904. The Adoians became refugees from the Turkish invasion; Gorky himself left Van in 1915 and arrived in the United States about March 1, 1920. He stayed with relatives in Watertown, Massachusetts, and with his father, who had settled in Providence, Rhode Island. By 1922 he lived in Watertown and taught at the New School of Design in Boston. In 1925 he moved to New York and changed his name to Arshile Gorky. He entered the Grand Central School of Art in New York as a student but soon became an instructor of drawing; from 1926 to 1931 he was a member of the faculty. Throughout the 1920s Gorky's painting was influenced by Cézanne, Braque, and, above all, Picasso.

In 1930 Gorky's work was included in a group show at The Museum of Modern Art in New York. During the thirties he associated closely with Stuart Davis, John Graham, and Willem de Kooning; he shared a studio with De Kooning late in the decade. Gorky's first one-man show took place at the Mellon Galleries in Philadelphia in 1931. From 1935 to 1937 he worked under the WPA Federal Art Project on murals for Newark Airport. His involvement with the WPA continued into 1941. Gorky's first one-man show in New York was held at the Boyer Galleries in 1938. The San Francisco Museum of Art exhibited his work in 1941.

In the 1940s he was profoundly affected by the work of the European Surrealists, particularly Miró, André Masson, and Matta. By 1944 he had met André Breton and become friends with other Surrealist emigrés in this country. Gorky's first exhibition at the Julien Levy Gallery in New York took place in 1945. From 1942 to 1948 he worked for part of each year in the countryside of Connecticut or Virginia. A succession of personal tragedies, including a fire in his studio which destroyed much of his work, a serious operation, and an automobile accident, preceded Gorky's death by suicide on July 21, 1948, in Sherman, Connecticut.

85. UNTITLED. 1943

Wax crayon and pencil on paper, 20 × 26¾ in. (50.8 × 67.9 cm.)
Gift, Rook McCulloch, 1977

In the 1940s Gorky executed hundreds of drawings in mixed media that were not specifically related to oil paintings. He worked from nature at his in-laws' farm in Hamilton, Virginia, during the summers of 1943, 1944, and 1946. Gorky investigated and inventively incorporated myriad natural forms in his work: leaves, petals, seed pods, stalks, plants, fields, rocks, and water. The genesis or transmutation of biomorphic forms and the intensification of imagery originated, at least in part, from the artist's concentration on details of visual experience.

This untitled crayon and pencil drawing dated 1943 is distinguished by a very dark and heavily worked background, which is contrasted with brilliant color at the upper and lower right and an openness at the center of the composition. Pencil lines accentuate contours of rounded, flower-like forms and spiky details. Gorky has applied isolated areas of green, red, orange, and black crayon. His interpretation of nature is both lyrical and associative; his forms are delicate, fluid, and incisive.

WILLEM DE KOONING

b. 1904. Willem de Kooning was born on April 24, 1904, in Rotterdam. From 1916 to 1925 he studied at night at the Academie voor Beeldende Kunsten en Technische Wetenschappen, Rotterdam, while apprenticing to a commercial art and decorating firm and later working for an art director. In 1924 he visited museums in Belgium and studied further in Brussels and Antwerp. De Kooning came to the United States in 1926 and settled briefly in Hoboken, New Jersey. He worked as a house painter before moving, in 1927, to New York, where he met John Graham, Stuart Davis, and Gorky. He worked at commercial art and various odd jobs until 1935–36, when he was employed in the mural and easel divisions of the WPA Federal Art Project. Thereafter he painted full time. In the late 1930s his abstract as well as figurative work was primarily influenced by the Cubism and Surrealism of Picasso and also of Gorky, with whom he shared a studio.

In 1938 De Kooning started his first series of Women, a subject that would become a major recurrent theme. During the 1940s he participated in group shows with other Abstract Expressionists—artists who would later form the New York School. De Kooning's first one-man show took place at the Egan Gallery in New York in 1948 and included a number of the allover black-and-white abstractions which he had initiated in 1946 and which subsequently established his reputation as a major artist. The Women of the early 1950s were followed by abstract urban landscapes, parkways, rural landscapes, and, in the 1960s, a new group of Women.

In 1968 De Kooning visited the Netherlands for the first time since 1926 for the opening of his major retrospective at the Stedelijk Museum in Amsterdam. In Rome in 1969 he executed his first sculptures—figures modeled in clay and later cast in bronze—and in 1970–71 he began a series of life-size figures. In 1974 the Walker Art Center in Minneapolis organized a show of De Kooning's drawings and sculpture that traveled throughout the United States, and in 1978 The Solomon R. Guggenheim Museum mounted an important exhibition of his recent work. In 1979 De Kooning and Eduardo Chillida received the Andrew W. Mellon Prize, which was accompanied by an exhibition at the Museum of Art, Carnegie Institute, in Pittsburgh. De Kooning lives in The Springs, East Hampton, Long Island, where he settled in 1963.

86. COMPOSITION. 1955

Oil, enamel, and charcoal on canvas, 79⅛ × 69⅛ in.
(201 × 175.6 cm.)
Acquired 1955

Throughout his career De Kooning has worked in both abstract and figurative modes. His abstractions of the late 1940s culminated in pictures like *Asheville*, 1949 (The Phillips Collection, Washington, D.C.), and *Excavation*, 1950 (Collection The Art Institute of Chicago). At approximately the same time De Kooning began a series of paintings of women that occupied him for several years and is probably best exemplified by *Woman I*, 1950–52 (Collection The Museum of Modern Art, New York). By early 1955 the figure gradually dissolved into an abstraction that nevertheless retained compositional elements of the earlier paintings of women. Completed by March 1955, *Composition* belongs to the period of transition from figure to landscape to abstraction. As early as 1953 the artist perceptively commented on his work that "the landscape is in the Woman and there is Woman in the landscapes." (*Willem de Kooning,* exh. cat., New York, 1968, p. 100.)

While related to urban landscapes such as *Police Gazette* of 1954–55 and *Gotham News* of 1955–56, the Guggenheim's *Composition* contains suggestions of female anatomy displaced and ambiguously rearranged on the picture plane. De Kooning does not focus solely on the two basic red forms but on the spaces between these shapes as well. Any resulting opposition between surface areas has been resolved through the use of color, the heavily brushed painted surface, and the heroic function of line.

JACKSON POLLOCK 1912–1956. Paul Jackson Pollock was born on January 28, 1912, in Cody, Wyoming. He grew up in Arizona and California and in 1928 began to study painting at the Manual Arts High School in Los Angeles. In the autumn of 1930 Pollock came to New York and studied under Thomas Hart Benton at the Art Students League. Benton encouraged him throughout the succeeding decade. By the early 1930s he knew and admired the murals of José Clemente Orozco and Diego Rivera. Much of Pollock's time was spent in New York, where he settled permanently in 1935 and worked on the WPA Federal Art Project from 1935 to 1942. In 1936 he worked in David Alfaro Siqueiros's experimental workshop in New York.

Pollock's first one-man show was held at Peggy Guggenheim's Art of This Century gallery in New York in 1943. Mrs. Guggenheim gave him a contract which lasted through 1947, permitting him to devote all his time to painting. Prior to 1947 Pollock's depiction of mythical or totemic figures as archetypes of the human subconscious reflected the influence of Surrealism. The year 1947 marks the beginning of his mature style: the large unprimed canvases covered with multicolored skeins of dripped paint, at once evoking the meanderings of the subconscious mind and emphasizing the primacy of paint and the force of spontaneous gesture. By 1951 Pollock's paintings, while remaining dynamically fluid, were limited to black and white and had become more sparse and austere.

From the autumn of 1945, when Lee Krasner and Pollock were married, they lived in The Springs, East Hampton. Pollock participated in the Venice Biennale in 1950. His work was widely known and exhibited, but the artist never traveled outside the United States. He was killed in an automobile accident August 11, 1956, in The Springs.

87. OCEAN GREYNESS. 1953
Oil on canvas, 57¾ × 90⅛ in. (146.7 × 229 cm.)
Acquired 1954

Ocean Greyness belongs to Pollock's late work: thus, it postdates his development of poured and dripped paint (1947–50) which culminated in monumental examples. Pollock's innovative and now famous technique involved working from all sides around a canvas placed directly on the floor. He created an allover composition that, by not focusing on a single point, seemed to defy the limits of the canvas. Not only the freedom of spontaneous gesture in dripping and flinging paint but also the energetic movements of the artist's body

were considered manifestations of the creative act of painting.

In *Ocean Greyness* the complexity of linear patterning is augmented by densely worked shapes articulated with a brush. This awareness of concrete forms, the emergent imagery of eyes, reverts to his earlier work. Pollock's explicit reference to the ocean recalls his seascapes from the late 1930s, has specifically Jungian connotations, and reappears in such coeval pictures as *The Deep* (Collection Musée National d'Art Moderne, Paris), *Sleeping Effort* (Collection Washington University, St. Louis), and *Greyed Rainbow* (Collection The Art Institute of Chicago). In *Ocean Greyness* the surface pulsates with rhythmic energy. The turbulence is emotional rather than merely oceanic.

MARK ROTHKO

1903–1970. Marcus Rothkowitz was born in Dvinsk, Russia, on September 25, 1903. In 1913 he left Russia and settled with the rest of his family in Portland, Oregon. Rothko attended Yale University in New Haven on a scholarship from 1921 to 1923. That year he left Yale without receiving a degree and moved to New York. In 1925 he studied under Max Weber at the Art Students League. He participated in his first group exhibition at the Opportunity Galleries in New York in 1928. During the early 1930s Rothko became close friends with Milton Avery and Adolph Gottlieb. His first one-man show took place at the Museum of Art in Portland in 1933.

Rothko's first one-man exhibition in New York was held at the Contemporary Arts Gallery in 1933. In 1935 he was a founding member of The Ten, a group of artists dedicated to the principles of abstraction and Expressionism. He executed easel paintings for the WPA Federal Art Project from 1936 to 1937. By 1936 Rothko had become acquainted with Barnett Newman. In the early forties he worked closely with Gottlieb, developing a painting style with mythological content, simple flat shapes, and imagery inspired by Primitive art. By mid-decade his work incorporated Surrealist techniques and images. Peggy Guggenheim gave Rothko a one-man show at her Art of This Century gallery in New York in 1945.

In 1947 and 1949 Rothko taught at the California School of Fine Arts, San Francisco, where Clyfford Still was a fellow instructor. Together with William Baziotes, David Hare, and Robert Motherwell, Rothko founded the short-lived The Subjects of the Artist school in New York in 1948. The late forties to early fifties saw the emergence of his mature style in which frontal, luminous rectangles seem to hover on the canvas surface. In 1958 the artist began his first commission—a group of monumental paintings for the Four Seasons Restaurant in New York. The Museum of Modern Art, New York, gave Rothko an important one-man exhibition in 1961. He completed murals for Harvard University in 1962 and in 1964 accepted a mural commission for a chapel in Houston. Rothko took his own life in his New York studio on February 25, 1970. A year later the Rothko Chapel in Houston was dedicated. A major retrospective of his work was held at The Solomon R. Guggenheim Museum in 1978–79.

88. VIOLET, BLACK, ORANGE, YELLOW ON WHITE AND RED. 1949

Oil on canvas, 81½ × 66 in. (207 × 167.6 cm.)
Gift, Elaine and Werner Dannheisser and The Dannheisser Foundation, 1978

With paintings like *Violet, Black, Orange, Yellow on White and Red*, Rothko established the horizontal and vertical structure of his mature work. He has united color with space, light, and form. In his multiform paintings of a year or two earlier, he brought loosely organized color areas forward onto the picture plane. Tension resulted from colors pushing forward and pulling back. In 1949–50 Rothko succeeded in maintaining all color forms on a single plane. His luminous colors radiate from the canvas.

In the Guggenheim's painting the greater weight of the violet rectangle at the top is counteracted by the adjacent vertical red bars and balanced by the juxtaposition of orange and yellow below. Black interrupts the color rectangles, and the surrounding white paint frees the composition so it appears to float. Over the next two decades Rothko would refine and simplify the pictorial organization arrived at here. The intensity and warmth of the colors in the Guggenheim's painting would be developed to express a wide range of mood and emotion.

ADOLPH GOTTLIEB

1903–1974. Adolph Gottlieb was born on March 14, 1903, in New York. He studied at the Art Students League with John Sloan and Robert Henri in 1920. During a two-year period in Europe from 1921 to 1923 he attended the Académie de la Grande Chaumière, Paris, and other studio schools and traveled to Berlin and Munich. Returning to New York in 1923, Gottlieb subsequently finished high school and studied at Parsons School of Design; the Art Students League, where his friendship with Barnett Newman developed; Cooper Union; and the Educational Alliance. In 1930 his first one-man show took place at the Dudensing Gallery in New York. His close friendship with Milton Avery and Rothko began in the early thirties. From 1935 to 1940 he exhibited with The Ten. In 1936 Gottlieb worked in the easel division of the WPA Federal Art Project; the next year he moved to the desert near Tucson, Arizona. He returned to New York in 1939 and spent the summers from 1939 to 1946 in Gloucester, Massachusetts.

In 1941 Gottlieb had painted his first pictographs—compositions divided into irregular grids, each compartment of which is filled with archetypal, mythic, and symbolic images. Continuing to express universal themes, in 1951 he began imaginary landscapes in which the field is divided into two horizontal zones: sky, with a number of shapes floating above the horizon, and landscape or sea below. These elements were simplified in his Burst paintings of 1957 to the early 1970s. Here, on large color fields, a disc characteristically hovers above an explosive, calligraphic mass.

Associated with the New York School, Gottlieb exhibited extensively from the 1940s until his death. He was given one-man shows at The Jewish Museum, New York, in 1957, and at the Walker Art Center, Minneapolis, in 1963; the latter exhibition was presented later that same year at the São Paulo Bienal. In 1968 a retrospective of his work was organized jointly by The Solomon R. Guggenheim Museum and the Whitney Museum of American Art, New York. He spent summers in Provincetown, Massachusetts, from 1946 until 1960, when he moved to East Hampton, Long Island. Gottlieb died in New York on March 4, 1974.

89. MIST. 1961

Oil on canvas, 72 × 48 in. (182.9 × 121.9 cm.)
Gift, Susan Morse Hilles, 1978

Gottlieb's distinctive color harmonies, forcefulness of imagery, and strong verticality of composition, already evident in the early fifties, are simplified and intensified in *Mist*. As its title implies, the palette consists of delicate nuances ranging from white and pale gray to blackish gray. A white circular form is diffused into a surrounding aura; it hovers over a vigorously painted, dynamic black shape. This division of the canvas into upper and lower segments remains constant in Gottlieb's Burst paintings (the earliest of which dates from 1957). He was interested in exploring the infinite and peculiar variations on the relationship between top and bottom elements of his compositions. Through the reduction of means, his images acquire a commanding presence.

FRANZ KLINE 1910–1962.

Franz Josef Kline was born on May 23, 1910, in Wilkes-Barre, Pennsylvania. While enrolled at Boston University he took art classes at the Boston Art Students League from 1931 to 1935. In 1935 Kline went to London and attended Heatherley's Art School from 1936 to 1938. He settled permanently in New York in 1939. Kline was fortunate to have the financial support and friendship of two patrons, Dr. Theodore J. Edlich, Jr., and I. David Orr, both of whom commissioned numerous portraits and bought many other works from him. During the late 1930s and 1940s Kline painted cityscapes and landscapes of the coal-mining district where he was raised, and executed commissioned murals and portraits. In this period he received awards in several National Academy of Design Annuals.

In 1943 Kline met De Kooning at Conrad Marca-Relli's studio and within the next few years also met Pollock. Kline's interest in Japanese art began at this time. His mature abstract style, characterized by bold gestural strokes of fast-drying black and white enamels, developed about 1949–50. His first one-man exhibition was held at the Egan Gallery in New York in 1950. Soon after, he was recognized as a major figure in the emerging Abstract Expressionist New York School. Although Kline was best known for his black-and-white paintings, he also worked extensively in color from the mid-1950s to the end of his life.

The artist spent a month in Europe in 1960 and traveled mostly in Italy. In the decade before his death, he was included in major international exhibitions, for example the 1956 and 1960 Venice Biennale presentations and the 1957 São Paulo Bienal, and won a number of important prizes. Kline died on May 13, 1962, in New York. The Gallery of Modern Art in Washington, D.C., organized a memorial exhibition of his work that same year. In 1963–64 The International Council of The Museum of Modern Art circulated a Kline retrospective in Europe and in 1968 the Whitney Museum of American Art in New York organized a retrospective that traveled in the United States.

90. PAINTING NO. 7. 1952
Oil on canvas, 57½ × 81¾ in. (146 × 207.6 cm.)
Acquired 1954

The artist has selected an essentially horizontal format where the verticals on the left reinforce the impenetrable blocklike shape at the right. He used housepainters' brushes in varying widths and commercially prepared house paints. Although some canvases may look spontaneous, Kline's paintings were not done at one time but evolved gradually as he repainted, shifted, and changed edges. Working on several canvases at a time, he allowed the paint to dry and kept the black and white areas separate.

It is significant that the artist arrived at his mature style—with its broad directional strokes—about 1949–50, after enlarging one of his sketches with a Bell-Opticon projector. The resulting change of scale obviously had wide ramifications. In working out the compositions of his paintings, he usually made sketches on pages of a telephone book or, less often, on newspaper. However, no studies for *Painting No. 7* have come to light.

Kline did not consider his paintings as black figures on white grounds but as a conflict between the white and black that resolved itself into a final unity. During the late forties and early fifties, a number of other painters including Pollock, Barnett Newman, De Kooning, and Motherwell experimented with restricting their palettes to black and white. For Kline the reduction of color was a way of concentrating on the essentials: this is evident in the stability and inevitability of the forms in *Painting No. 7*.

RICHARD DIEBENKORN b. 1922. Richard Clifford Diebenkorn was born on April 22, 1922, in Portland, Oregon. The family moved to San Francisco in 1924. Diebenkorn studied at Stanford University in Palo Alto from 1940 to 1943; he then transferred to the University of California at Berkeley and graduated from there in 1943. In 1946, after military service, he enrolled at the California School of Fine Arts, San Francisco, where David Park, Elmer Bischoff, and Hassel Smith were teachers. That year Diebenkorn moved to Woodstock, New York, where he became acquainted with Philip Guston and Bradley Walker Tomlin. He also met Kline at this time.

In 1947 Diebenkorn returned to California, taught drawing at the California School of Fine Arts, and saw the work of Clyfford Still. His first one-man exhibition was at the California Palace of the Legion of Honor, San Francisco, in 1948, the year he met Rothko and was introduced to De Kooning's work. In 1950–51 he enrolled in the M.F.A. program at the University of New Mexico at Albuquerque and began his Albuquerque paintings. Deeply moved by the 1952 Matisse exhibition in Los Angeles, Diebenkorn was inspired that same year to begin the vibrantly colored Urbana paintings in Illinois. In 1953, while teaching at the California College of Arts and Crafts, Oakland, Diebenkorn began his Berkeley paintings. From 1955 to the mid-sixties the artist painted in a figurative manner. He participated in the 1955 São Paulo Bienal and was given a retrospective in 1960 at the Pasadena Art Museum. In 1964–65 Diebenkorn traveled to the Soviet Union and saw the Matisses in the Shchukin and Hermitage collections.

By 1967 he had moved to the Ocean Park section of Santa Monica and started to paint his large, abstract Ocean Park canvases. Diebenkorn was included in the 1968 Venice Biennale and was given a one-man show in 1969 at the Los Angeles County Museum of Art. In 1975 the San Francisco Museum of Art presented a large exhibition of his Ocean Park paintings, and in 1976 the Albright-Knox Art Gallery, Buffalo, organized a major Diebenkorn retrospective which traveled in the United States into 1977. He was given a one-man show at the 1978 Venice Biennale. Diebenkorn still lives and works in Santa Monica.

91. OCEAN PARK NO. 96. 1977

Oil on canvas, 93⅛ × 85⅛ in. (236.3 × 216.1 cm.) Purchased with the aid of funds from the National Endowment for the Arts in Washington, D.C., a Federal Agency; matching funds donated by Mr. and Mrs. Stuart M. Speiser and Louis and Bessie Adler Foundation, Inc., Seymour M. Klein, President, 1977

Ocean Park No. 96 is one of a series of large, totally abstract paintings that Diebenkorn started in 1967 and is still working on today. Ocean Park is the name of a section of Santa Monica where the artist's studio is located. The light-filled colors suggest sky, sea, sand, and earth. In fact, Diebenkorn has stated that temperamentally he has always been a landscape painter.

In *Ocean Park No. 96* the composition is governed by a reiteration of rectangles formed by the intersection of horizontal and vertical lines which occurs primarily at the upper right and left corners. Diagonal accents cut across color areas. Diebenkorn has partially painted over certain lines to suggest continuity rather than explicit partitioning. His Ocean Park pictures are either square or, as here, vertical in format. The subtle differentiation in width and length of color zones and the concern with spatial implications of structure are characteristic of the series as a whole.

ISAMU NOGUCHI

b. 1904. Isamu Noguchi was born on November 17, 1904, in Los Angeles. His Japanese father was a poet and his American mother a writer. In 1906 the family moved to Japan. He was sent to Indiana for schooling in 1918, and in 1922 he apprenticed to the sculptor Gutzon Borglum in Connecticut. For the next two years he was a premedical student at Columbia University and took sculpture classes at the Leonardo da Vinci School in New York. Noguchi decided to become an artist and left Columbia in 1925. A John Simon Guggenheim Foundation Fellowship in 1927 enabled him to go to Paris, where he worked as Brancusi's studio assistant. In Paris he became friendly with Calder, Jules Pascin, and Stuart Davis. Noguchi returned to New York in 1928 and the following year showed abstract sculpture in his first one-man show at the Eugene Schoen Gallery.

In 1930 Noguchi traveled in Europe and the Orient, studying calligraphy in China and pottery in Japan. In New York during the early thirties he associated with Gorky, Chaim Gross, John Graham, and Moses and Raphael Soyer and introduced social content into his work. He began to design playgrounds, furniture, and theater decor, executing the first of numerous sets for Martha Graham. Noguchi spent six months in 1941–42 in a Japanese-American relocation camp. In 1949 he was given a one-man show at the Egan Gallery, New York. In Japan in 1950–51 he designed gardens, bridges, and monuments and developed his *akari* (paper lanterns). He showed at the Stable Gallery in New York in 1954 and 1959.

In 1961 Noguchi moved to Long Island City. His first one-man exhibition in Paris was held at the Galerie Claude Bernard in 1964. The Whitney Museum of American Art, New York, honored him with a major retrospective in 1968. Throughout the seventies Noguchi continued to make large outdoor sculpture and fountains. A comprehensive show of his sculpture, theater sets, and environmental works took place in 1978 at the Walker Art Center in Minneapolis. Noguchi now lives in New York City and spends part of each year in Japan.

92. THE CRY. 1959
Balsa wood on steel base, 84 × 30 × 18 in. (213.4 × 76.2 × 45.7 cm.)
Acquired 1966

In the late 1950s, while continuing to work in cast-iron and marble, Noguchi explored the possibilities inherent in lightweight materials. He sought to convey a sense of lightness and weightlessness in aluminum pieces such as *Lunar* and in balsa wood sculptures such as *The Cry,* both in the Guggenheim Museum collection. Noguchi had occasionally employed balsa, one of the lightest woods, since the 1940s. In *The Cry* he presents abstract shapes in asymmetrical alignment: biomorphic forms seem to float effortlessly in space. Not only does the lateral element appear precariously suspended, but it is attached so it can move very slightly, responding to air currents and vibrations.

In 1962, as Noguchi's interest in mass and gravity evolved, he decided to have several wood pieces cast in bronze. Bronze versions of *The Cry* are in the Albright-Knox Art Gallery in Buffalo, the San Francisco Museum of Modern Art, and four other collections.

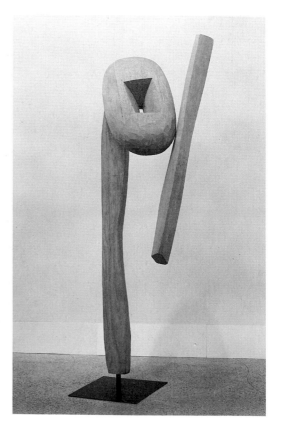

184

LOUISE NEVELSON b. 1899.

Louise Berliawsky was born on September 23, 1899, in Kiev, Russia. By 1905 her family had emigrated to the United States and settled in Rockland, Maine. In 1920 she married Charles Nevelson and moved to New York. At this time she studied visual and performing arts, including dramatics with Frederick Kiesler. Nevelson enrolled at the Art Students League in 1928 and also studied with Hilla Rebay. During this period she was introduced to the work of Duchamp and Picasso. In 1931, while traveling in Europe, she briefly attended Hofmann's school in Munich. Nevelson returned to New York in 1932 and assisted Diego Rivera on murals he was executing under the WPA Federal Art Project. Shortly thereafter, in the early thirties, she turned to sculpture. Between 1933 and 1936 her work was included in numerous group exhibitions in New York, and in 1937 she joined the WPA as a teacher for the Educational Alliance School of Art.

Nevelson's first one-woman show took place in 1941 at the Nierendorf Gallery in New York. In 1943 she began her Farm assemblages, in which pieces of wood and found objects were incorporated. She studied etching with Stanley William Hayter at his Atelier 17 in New York in 1947 and in 1949–50 worked in marble and terra-cotta and executed her totemic *Game Figures*. Nevelson showed in 1953 and 1955 at the Grand Central Moderns Gallery in New York. In 1957 she made her first reliefs in shadow boxes as well as her first wall. Two years later Nevelson participated in her first important museum exhibition, "Sixteen Americans," at The Museum of Modern Art in New York, and the Martha Jackson Gallery gave her a one-woman show. She was included in the Venice Biennale in 1962.

Nevelson was elected President of National Artists Equity in 1965 and the following year she became Vice-President of the International Association of Artists. Her first major museum retrospective took place in 1967 at the Whitney Museum of American Art in New York. Princeton University commissioned Nevelson to create a monumental outdoor steel sculpture in 1969, the same year The Museum of Fine Arts, Houston, gave her a solo exhibition. Other Nevelson shows took place in 1970 at the Whitney Museum and in 1973 at the Walker Art Center in Minneapolis. Nevelson lives and works in New York.

93. *LUMINOUS ZAG: NIGHT.* 1971

Painted wood, 105 boxes, total 120 × 193 × 10¾ in. (304.8 × 490.3 × 27.3 cm.); each 16⅝ × 12⅝ × 10¾ in. (42.2 × 32 × 27.3 cm.)
Gift, Sidney Singer, 1977

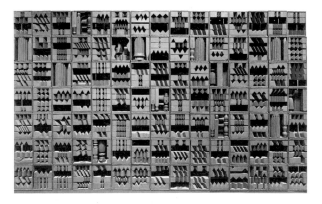

Nevelson has worked almost exclusively in wood and has chosen to paint her sculpture, thus obscuring the grain, color, and other inherent qualities of the material. The majority of her work is painted black, although many sculptures are completely white or gold. In large wall pieces such as *Luminous Zag: Night,* black paint unifies the large number of components and contributes an element of regularity to the multiplicity of shapes within the total composition. Nevelson's construction is seven boxes high and fifteen across; it reaches a height of ten feet and extends to sixteen feet in width. Within individual boxes she has variously arranged horizontal zigzag elements, columns, and balusters. *Luminous Zag: Night* has a strongly horizontal emphasis punctuated with occasional verticals. It is closely related to *Luminous Zag* (Collection The Pace Gallery, New York), a smaller coeval sculpture that also displays indented zigzag patterns. Working with her own formal vocabulary, Nevelson attains consistency through modular organization and the use of uniform color.

DAVID SMITH 1906–1965. David Roland Smith was born on March 9, 1906, in Decatur, Indiana. During high school he took a correspondence course with the Cleveland Art School. In 1924 Smith studied at Ohio University, Athens. He worked as an automobile welder and riveter in the summer of 1925. He then attended Notre Dame University for two weeks before moving to Washington, D.C. In 1926 Smith moved to New York, where he studied at the Art Students League with Richard Lahey and John Sloan and privately with Jan Matulka. In 1929 he met John Graham, who later introduced him to the welded steel sculpture of Picasso and Julio González. That same year he bought a farm in Bolton Landing near Lake George in upstate New York.

Gorky, De Kooning, Pollock, Jean Xceron, Stuart Davis, and Edgar Levy were his friends throughout the thirties. In the Virgin Islands in 1931–32 Smith made his first sculpture from pieces of coral. He began making all-metal sculpture in 1933, and in 1934 he set up a studio at the Terminal Iron Works in Brooklyn. In 1935–36 he visited France, Greece, England, and Russia. Upon his return to New York Smith began the *Medals for Dishonor*, antiwar medallions. In 1937 he made sculpture for the WPA Federal Art Project. His first one-man show of drawings and welded steel sculpture was held at Marion Willard's East River Gallery in New York in 1938.

In 1940 Smith settled permanently in Bolton Landing. From 1942 to 1944 he worked as a locomotive welder in Schenectady. A one-man show of his work took place at the Walker Art Center, Minneapolis, in 1941. Smith taught at Sarah Lawrence College, Bronxville, New York, from 1948 to 1950, and at Bennington College, Bennington, Vermont, and at other schools during the fifties. About 1951 he met Kenneth Noland. The Museum of Modern Art, New York, presented a Smith retrospective in 1957 and organized a major traveling exhibition of his work in 1961. In 1962, at the invitation of the Italian government, he went to Voltri, near Genoa, and executed twenty-seven sculptures for the Spoleto festival. In 1963 he began his Cubi series of monumental, geometric steel sculptures. David Smith died on May 23, 1965, in an automobile accident near Bennington. The Guggenheim Museum organized an exhibition of his work in 1969.

94. CUBI XXVII. March 1965
Stainless steel, 111⅜ × 87¾ × 34 in. (282.9 × 222.9 × 86.4 cm.)
Acquired 1967

Smith's Cubi series consists of twenty-eight sculptures of that title, all constructed in stainless steel. *Cubi XXVII* is the penultimate work of the theme, which began in 1963 and ended with the artist's death in May 1965. Like *Cubi XXIV*, which is dated December 8, 1964, and *Cubi XXVIII*, the Guggenheim's example assumes the appearance of a monumental gate. The geometric forms achieve an asymmetrical balance and greater stability than in many preceding Cubi, where shapes are placed precariously, one on top of another. For these sculptures Smith chose burnished, reflective surfaces that respond to the changing colors and light of their surroundings. The reflective properties deny the solidity and weight implied by the massive forms. The frontality of the composition indicates how the sculpture should be seen and relates it to the two-dimensionality of painting and drawing. Smith made sprayed pencil drawings for many of the Cubi, including the present example.

ROBERT RAUSCHENBERG

ROBERT RAUSCHENBERG b. 1925. Milton Rauschenberg, who was to become known as Bob in the 1940s, was born on October 22, 1925, in Port Arthur, Texas. He studied briefly at the University of Texas in 1942 before serving in the navy from 1942 to 1945. Under the G.I. Bill he attended the Kansas City Art Institute from 1947 until early 1948, when he went to Paris and enrolled at the Académie Julian. In the fall of 1948 he returned to the United States to study with Albers at Black Mountain College, Black Mountain, North Carolina. At Black Mountain he met John Cage and Merce Cunningham. In 1949 Rauschenberg moved to New York and studied at the Art Students League with Morris Kantor and Vaclav Vytlacil until 1952.

Rauschenberg experimented with photographic blueprints between 1949 and 1951. His first one-man show took place at Betty Parsons Gallery, New York, in 1951, and he produced all-black and all-white paintings in 1951–52. In 1952 the artist began his travels to Italy, France, Spain, and North Africa. He exhibited small objects and boxes in Rome and Florence before returning to New York in the spring of 1953. That same year he began a series of all-red paintings and made his famous anti-art gesture of erasing a De Kooning drawing. In this period Rauschenberg started to design sets and costumes for Cunningham's dance company as well as for Paul Taylor's.

From 1955 to 1959 Rauschenberg worked on "combines"—constructions, classifiable as neither painting nor sculpture, in which he incorporated objects (a stuffed goat, a bed, tires). During these years he worked closely with Jasper Johns, who, like himself, was influenced by Duchamp. In 1961 Rauschenberg made his first lithograph; he has subsequently incorporated the silk-screen process in many canvases and experimented with various printmaking techniques. In the mid-1960s he created his own dances and performances. Throughout the 1960s and 1970s he continued to explore new techniques and materials. In 1966 he cofounded E.A.T. (Experiments in Art and Technology), to promote cooperation between artists and engineers, and in 1970 established Change Inc., a foundation that provides financial aid to artists. In 1976–77 a major Rauschenberg retrospective organized by The National Collection of Fine Arts, Washington, D.C., traveled in the United States. Rauschenberg lives in New York and Captiva, an island off the Florida coast.

95. UNTITLED. 1963

Oil, silk screen, ink, metal, and plastic on canvas,
82 x 48 in. (208.3 × 121.9 cm.)
Purchased with funds contributed by Elaine and Werner Dannheisser
and The Dannheisser Foundation, 1982

To Rauschenberg "a pair of socks is no less suitable to make a painting with than wood, nails, turpentine, oil and fabric." (*Sixteen Americans,* exh. cat., New York, 1959, p. 58.) In the late 1950s Rauschenberg did indeed use socks and other radical materials, including stuffed animals, street refuse, and Coca-Cola bottles. In *Untitled,* amid patches of bright red, blue, orange, and white paint, he incorporated a metal box with vents and a plastic lid—three-dimensional elements projecting from the surface and giving the work a greater physical presence.

If this combine-painting appears toward the end of the period in which the artist created dissonance by using found objects, it stands at the beginning of his exploration of multiple, mechanically reproduced images. With photosensitive screens both Rauschenberg and Andy Warhol contemporaneously began to reproduce photographs in their paintings in order to abolish the romanticism of the unique and handmade. The photos here—of a Coca-Cola sign and of rockets blasting off (the latter an emblem of the excitement surrounding the Project Mercury space program)—steep this work in its era.

ANDY WARHOL 1928–1987.

Andrew Warhola was born on August 6, 1928, in Pittsburgh. He received his B.F.A. from the Carnegie Institute of Technology, Pittsburgh, in 1949. That same year he came to New York, where he soon became successful as a commercial artist and illustrator. During the 1950s Warhol's drawings were published in *Glamour* and other magazines and displayed in department stores; he became known for his illustrations of I. Miller shoes. In 1952 the Hugo Gallery in New York presented a show of Warhol's illustrations for Truman Capote's writings. He traveled in Europe and Asia in 1956.

By the early 1960s Warhol began to paint comic-strip characters and images derived from advertisements; this work was characterized by repetition of banal subjects such as Coca-Cola bottles and soup cans. He also painted celebrities at this time. Warhol's new painting was exhibited for the first time in 1962: initially at the Ferus Gallery in Los Angeles, then in a one-man show at the Stable Gallery in New York. By 1963 he had substituted a silk-screen process for hand painting. Working with assistants, he produced series of disasters, flowers, cows, and portraits as well as three-dimensional facsimile Brillo boxes and cartons of other well-known household products.

Starting in the mid-1960s at The Factory, his New York studio, Warhol concentrated on making films that were marked by repetition and an emphasis on boredom. In the early 1970s he began to paint again, returning to gestural brushwork, and produced monumental portraits of Mao Tse-tung, commissioned portraits, and the Hammer and Sickle series. He also became interested in writing: his autobiography, *The Philosophy of Andy Warhol (From A to B and Back Again)*, was published in 1975, and The Factory publishes *Interview* magazine. A major retrospective of Warhol's work organized by the Pasadena Art Museum in 1970 traveled in the United States and abroad. Warhol died in New York on February 22, 1987.

96. ORANGE DISASTER. 1963
Acrylic and silk-screen enamel on canvas, 106 × 81½ in. (269.2 × 207 cm.)
Gift, Harry N. Abrams Family Collection, 1974

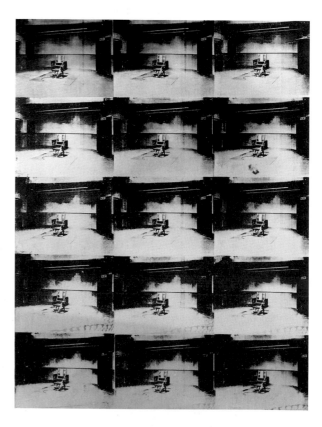

Orange Disaster is one of several paintings featuring multiple images of an electric chair that Warhol executed in the same format but different colors (for example, *Lavender Disaster* of 1964). The artist employed the same photograph—as a single image—in a series of Little Electric Chairs in 1965 and in the Big Electric Chairs of 1967. Moreover, *Orange Disaster* is related to a number of other death or disaster themes of the period, all based on news photographs: car crashes, suicides, race riots, hospital images.

To produce this work Warhol used a photomechanical silk-screen process, whereby the artist is significantly removed from the act of painting. In *Orange Disaster* one image is replicated fifteen times, but each frame in the sequence varies somewhat because of irregularities in the application of paint. The choice of such an emotionally charged subject as the electric chair is in marked contrast to the anonymity, detachment, and mechanical repetition of Warhol's method. In general, serial imagery and the single color scheme reinforce the banality of Warhol's subjects. It is ironic that the selection of images directly from the mass media and popular culture should become the mark of individuality in his art.

ROY LICHTENSTEIN b. 1923.

Roy Lichtenstein was born on October 27, 1923, in New York. During the summer of 1939 he studied with Reginald Marsh at the Art Students League, and in 1940 he entered the School of Fine Arts at Ohio State University, in Columbus, where Hoyt L. Sherman was his teacher. After military service from 1943 to January 1946 Lichtenstein returned to Ohio State, receiving his B.F.A. in 1946 and M.F.A. in 1949. He remained there as an instructor from 1949 to 1951. In 1951 his first one-man show took place in New York at the Carlebach Gallery. That same year Lichtenstein moved to Cleveland, where he continued to paint while supporting himself as an engineering draftsman until 1957. Subsequently, he taught at the State University of New York, Oswego (1957–60), and at Douglass College, Rutgers University, New Brunswick, New Jersey (1960–63). In 1963 he moved to New York and began to paint full time.

Lichtenstein progressed from depicting Americana subjects of the Old West to an Abstract Expressionist mode in the late 1950s. While teaching at Rutgers he met Allan Kaprow, Claes Oldenburg, Jim Dine, Lucas Samaras, George Segal, and Robert Whitman, all of whom were significant in the development of Happenings. At this time Lichtenstein was a seminal figure in the Pop Art movement. In 1961 he began using Ben Day printing dots for the first time, painting comic-strip subjects, isolated household objects, and images from advertisements. Subsequently, he produced stylized landscapes (1964–65), parodies of Abstract Expressionist brushstrokes (1965–66), Pop versions of paintings by modern masters such as Cézanne, Mondrian, Monet, and Picasso, and compositions based on Art Deco motifs and WPA murals (1966–70). In the 1970s he painted mirrors and entablatures in a more abstract style. Lichtenstein has also made sculpture in polychrome ceramics as well as in brass and aluminum and has produced numerous silk-screen prints. Since 1962 he has shown regularly at the Leo Castelli Gallery in New York, and in 1966 he participated in the Venice Biennale. Major exhibitions of his work were organized by the Pasadena Art Museum in 1967 and The Solomon R. Guggenheim Museum in 1969. Since 1970 Lichtenstein has lived in Southampton, Long Island.

97. PREPAREDNESS. 1968

Magna on canvas, three panels, each 120 × 72 in.
(304.8 × 183 cm.)
Acquired 1969

As Lichtenstein has said, *Preparedness* is "a muralesque painting about our military-industrial complex." The artist deliberately chose the title for its "call-to-arms quality" and fully intended direct social comment (D. Waldman, *Roy Lichtenstein*, New York, 1971, pp. 26–27). Painted late in 1968 at the height of the Vietnam War, *Preparedness* shows, at the left, factories and smokestacks, a prerequisite for mobilization of the military. In the central panel a row of helmeted soldiers dominates a scene that includes a display of girders and gears and a hand holding a hammer, while, in the right panel, a soldier and an airplane window complete the composition. The three large panels are united by strong diagonals and geometric compositional elements, by the use of primary colors, and by the use of Ben Day dots that uniformly articulate the canvases.

Lichtenstein wanted to make a statement about heroic compositions that would carry with it strong overtones of the 1930s. Beginning in 1966 the artist explored the stylistic possibilities of reinterpreting the motifs of the 1930s as seen from the vantage point of the late 1960s, an interest perhaps best exemplified by Lichtenstein's sculpture.

The painting *Study for Preparedness* (Ludwig Collection, Wallraf-Richartz-Museum, Cologne) is remarkably similar to the final version in the Guggenheim in all respects but size. There is also a colored drawing of the same composition in a New York private collection.

MORRIS LOUIS

1912–1962. Morris Louis Bernstein was born on November 28, 1912, in Baltimore. From 1929 to 1933 he studied at the Maryland Institute of Fine and Applied Arts on a scholarship but left shortly before completing the program. He worked at various odd jobs to support himself while painting and in 1935 served as President of the Baltimore Artists' Association. From 1936 to 1940 Louis lived in New York, where he worked in the easel division of the WPA Federal Art Project. During this period he knew David Alfaro Siqueiros, Gorky, and Jack Tworkov, and he dropped his last name. He returned to Baltimore in 1940 and taught privately. In 1948 he started to use Magna acrylic paints. In 1952 Louis moved to Washington, D.C., where he taught at the Washington Workshop Center of the Arts and met fellow instructor Noland, who became a close friend. Louis's first one-man show took place at the Workshop Center Art Gallery in 1953.

In 1953 he and Noland visited Helen Frankenthaler's New York studio: there they saw and were greatly impressed by her stain painting *Mountains and Sea* of 1952. Upon their return to Washington, Louis and Noland together experimented with various techniques of paint application. In 1954 Louis produced his mature Veil paintings, which were characterized by overlapping, superimposed layers of transparent color poured and stained into sized or unsized canvas. Louis's first one-man show in New York was held at the Martha Jackson Gallery in 1957. He destroyed many of the paintings in this show but resumed work on the Veils in 1958–59. These were followed by Florals and Columns (1960), Unfurleds (1960–61)—where rivulets of more opaque, intense color flow from both sides of large white fields—and Stripe paintings (late 1961–62). Louis died in Washington, D.C., on September 7, 1962. A memorial exhibition of his work was held at The Solomon R. Guggenheim Museum in 1963. Major Louis exhibitions were also organized by the Museum of Fine Arts, Boston, in 1967, and the National Collection of Fine Arts, Washington, D.C., in 1976.

98. SARABAND. 1959

Acrylic resin on canvas, 101⅛ × 149 in.
(257 × 378.5 cm.)
Acquired 1964

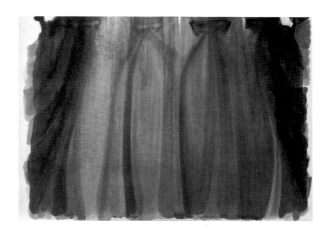

Louis's large painting, *Saraband*, demonstrates his innovative manner of pouring thinned acrylic paint on unprimed cotton duck canvas. Here, successive washes of bright colors were followed by a final dark layer. The canvas has absorbed the colors, creating a stained, translucent surface. Like Frankenthaler, Louis expanded upon Pollock's stylistic and technical breakthrough.

Louis's first Veil paintings date from 1954; he returned to them in 1958–59. These canvases are often hung so that the paint touches the bottom edge and the white margin is at the top. *Saraband*, however, was not hung this way during the artist's lifetime, and the position of his signature confirms how he meant it to be seen. In *Saraband* and other paintings of the series, veils of color extend almost to the perimeters and fill the great expanse of canvas. Louis has superseded the traditional figure-ground relationship and eliminated painterly gesture and drawing per se. He has united color, form, texture, and movement in a totally abstract, rhythmic pictorial surface.

ELLSWORTH KELLY b. 1923. Ellsworth Kelly was born on May 31, 1923, in Newburgh, New York. He studied at Pratt Institute, Brooklyn, in 1941–42. After serving in the military in a camouflage unit in Europe from 1943 to 1945 he attended the School of the Museum of Fine Arts, Boston, from 1946 to 1948. In 1948 Kelly went to France and enrolled at the Ecole des Beaux-Arts in Paris under the G.I. Bill. In France he studied Romanesque art and architecture and Byzantine art; here he was introduced to Surrealism and Neo-Plasticism, which led him to experiment with automatic drawing and geometric abstraction. In 1950 Kelly met Arp and that same year began to make collages, arranged by chance, and wood reliefs. He met other artists in Paris including Brancusi, Vantongerloo, Picabia, and Sophie Taeuber-Arp. Kelly taught at the American School in Paris in 1950–51. His first one-man show took place at the Galerie Arnaud, Paris, in 1951. In 1951–52 he worked in Sanary in the south of France.

Kelly returned to the United States in 1954; he moved to Coenties Slip in lower Manhattan, where his neighbors were Agnes Martin, Robert Indiana, and Jack Youngerman, who had been a close friend in Paris. His first one-man show in New York was held at the Betty Parsons Gallery in 1956. Since the early 1950s Kelly has alternated between basic hard-edged elements and curved shapes. He uses brilliant, unmodulated colors as well as black and white and variations of gray in single-canvas formats and compositions of two or more panels. In addition to his abstract work Kelly has made many contour drawings of plants. He has also worked extensively in sculpture, collage, and various print mediums. The artist has executed a number of important public commissions, including a mural for UNESCO in Paris in 1969. Among his extensive exhibitions in the United States and abroad are important one-man shows at the Albright-Knox Art Gallery, Buffalo, 1972; The Museum of Modern Art, New York, 1973; and The Metropolitan Museum of Art, New York, 1979. Kelly now lives in Chatham, New York.

99. BLUE, GREEN, YELLOW, ORANGE, RED
1966
Acrylic on canvas, five panels, each 60 × 48 in.
(152.3 × 121.9 cm.)
Acquired 1967

As early as 1952–53 Kelly made innovative paintings by juxtaposing a series of individual, vertical panels that are identical in size but different in color. However, when he returned to this format in 1966, his selection of colors became more systematic: for example, in this painting the primary colors, blue, yellow, and red, alternate from left to right with the complementaries, green and orange. By increasing the scale of unmodulated expanses of bright, highly saturated hues and eliminating any trace of brushwork, Kelly makes color area synonymous with the shape of the canvas. Each of the five horizontally aligned panels, while distinguished by its color, functions simultaneously as an integral unit within the whole.

Although the title encourages the viewer to read the panels from left to right, it is not necessary to see them in a particular order and the colors may be visually grouped and regrouped in several ways. Furthermore, the large scale forces the viewer to remain at a distance to see the work in its entirety. An intensification and vibration of color occurs where one panel adjoins the next; yet the five different color values are remarkably balanced and hold the same flat plane. Kelly is generally considered reductive in his concentration on pure shape, line, and color. However, his exploration of these basic elements is decidedly sensuous rather than austere.

191

RICHARD ESTES b. 1936. Richard William Estes was born in Kewanee, Illinois, on May 14, 1936. He grew up in Sheffield and Evanston. From 1952 to 1956 Estes studied at The Art Institute of Chicago and admired the works of El Greco, Degas, and Seurat. In 1956 he supported himself by doing paste-ups and mechanicals for various publishing and advertising firms. Estes moved to New York in 1959 and continued to take jobs as a graphic artist. In 1962 he lived and painted in Spain. For the next few years Estes did free-lance assignments and was employed by a magazine publisher in New York. In 1966 he began to devote himself full time to painting. He painted in a highly realistic style, often from his own photographs and charcoal or watercolor sketches.

Estes's first one-man show was held at the Allan Stone Gallery in New York in 1968. The following year he was included in the Milwaukee Art Center's traveling exhibition "Directions 2: Aspects of a New Realism," and he was recognized as a major Photo-Realist painter. Estes participated in the 1970 Annual at the Whitney Museum of American Art, New York, and in the 1971 "Biennial Exhibition of Contemporary American Painting" at the Corcoran Gallery of Art, Washington, D.C. In 1972 his work was shown at the Venice Biennale and at "Documenta 5," in Kassel, Germany. The Museum of Contemporary Art in Chicago presented a one-man show of Estes's work in 1974. In 1978 the Museum of Fine Arts, Boston, organized an important Estes exhibition which traveled in the United States into 1979. The artist lives and works in New York and Northeast Harbor, Maine.

100. THE SOLOMON R. GUGGENHEIM MUSEUM. Summer 1979

Oil on canvas, 31⅛ × 55⅛ in. (79 × 140 cm.) Purchased with the aid of funds from the National Endowment for the Arts in Washington, D.C., a Federal Agency; matching funds donated by Mr. and Mrs. Barrie M. Damson, 1979

As Estes began to formulate his ideas for a painting of the Guggenheim Museum early in 1979, he took dozens of color photographs from various exterior and interior points of view. By May the quality of light on the facade was significantly different from what it had been during the winter months. Especially on clear spring days just before sunset, the trees in Central Park cast distinct shadows on the building. From the rolls of film he shot in May, Estes selected three views upon which he based the composition. Comparison of the canvas with the site at Fifth Avenue and 88th Street reveals various differences—primarily adjustments in size, scale, and color.

It is the artist's usual practice to edit his photographs extensively and to combine several views of a scene into a composite. After he establishes the composition, he works slowly to achieve the desired clarity of light and the proper relationship between elements. *The Solomon R. Guggenheim Museum* is exceptional in Estes's work: it is the only time he set out to paint a specific, well-known building.

COLORPLATES

Gorky • De Kooning • Pollock • Rothko • Gottlieb • Kline • Diebenkorn • Noguchi • Nevelson • Smith • Rauschenberg • Warhol • Lichtenstein • Louis • Kelly • Estes

85. ARSHILE GORKY *Untitled.* 1943

86. WILLEM DE KOONING *Composition.* 1955

87. JACKSON POLLOCK *Ocean Greyness.* 1953

88. MARK ROTHKO *Violet, Black, Orange, Yellow on White and Red.* 1949

90. FRANZ KLINE *Painting No. 7.* 1952

91. RICHARD DIEBENKORN *Ocean Park No. 96.* 1977

92. ISAMU NOGUCHI *The Cry.* 1959

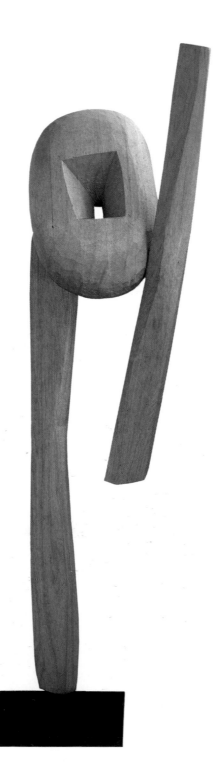

93. LOUISE NEVELSON *Luminous Zag: Night.* 1971

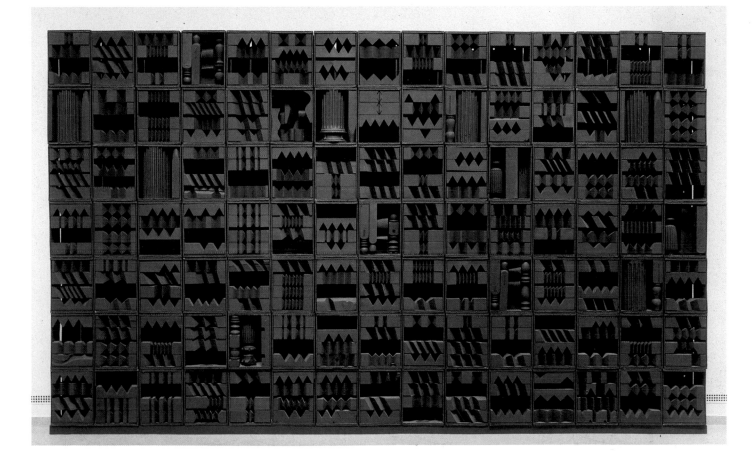

96. ANDY WARHOL *Orange Disaster.* 1963

97. ROY LICHTENSTEIN *Preparedness.* 1968

98. MORRIS LOUIS *Saraband.* 1959

99. ELLSWORTH KELLY *Blue, Green, Yellow, Orange, Red.* 1966

100. RICHARD ESTES *The Solomon R. Guggenheim Museum.* 1979

INDEX OF PLATES

PHOTOGRAPH CREDITS

COLOR (listed by plate number)

Geoffrey Clements, New York: 55; Carmelo Guadagno, New York: 1–3, 6, 9, 11, 14–18, 20, 25, 28, 30, 32, 33, 44, 46, 56, 62, 63, 65, 72, 76, 77, 81, 82, 84, 88, 89; Carmelo Guadagno and David Heald, New York: 4, 5, 7, 8, 19, 24, 29, 31, 38, 39, 45, 52, 64, 66, 78, 79, 87, 96–98, 100; David Heald, New York: 23, 27, 34, 36, 42, 47–49, 57, 58, 61, 70, 80, 95; Robert E. Mates, New York: 10, 12, 13, 21, 22, 26, 35, 37, 40, 41, 43, 50, 51, 53, 54, 59, 60, 67–69, 71, 73–75, 83, 85, 86, 90–94, 99.

BLACK AND WHITE (listed by page number)

All black-and-white photographs are by Robert E. Mates except for the following: Hannes Beckmann, New York: 7 (lower right), 9 (upper right); Roloff Beny, Rome: 13 (lower left); Mary Donlon, New York: 13 (upper left); Carmelo Guadagno, New York: 13 (lower right), 31, 117; Carmelo Guadagno and David Heald, New York: 12 (lower right), 188–90; David Heald, New York: 179, 187; Courtesy Hope Associates, Corp., New York: 8 (lower left); Marilyn Mazur, New York: 13 (upper right); Courtesy *Newsday*, Melville, N.Y.: 12 (upper right); William H. Short, Jr., Princeton, N.J.: 10 (left); Courtesy The Solomon R. Guggenheim Museum, New York: 7 (upper left, upper right, lower left), 8 (upper left, upper right, lower right), 12 (left); Waintrob-Budd, New York: 11 (upper left).